10C87

TRINITY AND ALL SAINTS
A COLLEGE OF THE UNIVERSITY OF LEEDS

L.R.S. LIBRARY

This book is due for return on or before the last date stamped below

This book is dedicated to the late Clifford Ellis, first Principal of Bath Academy of Art, who through his thinking and example had a profound influence upon a whole generation of art teachers.

THE ART
TEACHER'S
HANDBOOK

Robert Clement

HUTCHINSON

London Melbourne Sydney Auckland Johannesburg

Hutchinson Education

An imprint of Century Hutchinson Ltd

62–65 Chandos Place, London WC2N 4NW

Century Hutchinson South Africa (Pty) Ltd
PO Box 337, Bergvlei, 2012 South Africa

Century Hutchinson Australia Pty Ltd
PO Box 496, 16–22 Church Street, Hawthorn,
Victoria 3122, Australia

Century Hutchinson New Zealand Limited
PO Box 40-086, Glenfield, Auckland 10,
New Zealand

First published 1986
Reprinted 1986, 1987

© Robert Clement 1986

Typeset in Gill Sans by Rowland Phototypesetting Ltd
Bury St Edmunds, Suffolk

Printed and bound in Great Britain

British Library Cataloguing in Publication Data

Clement, Robert,
    The art teacher's handbook.
    1. Art – Study and teaching (Secondary) –
    Great Britain
    I. Title
    707'.1241   N365.G7

    ISBN 0 09 164181 0

CONTENTS

CONTENTS

ACKNOWLEDGEMENTS

I would like to thank Nigel Coulton for his patience and skill in preparing the photographs that illustrate this book.

In addition to all those teachers who have contributed so much to this publication through their work in schools, I would like to thank the following colleagues who in their different ways have made a very special contribution to my work — through their support, through their thinking and through so many intriguing and friendly arguments:

Maurice Barrett, *Senior Adviser, London Borough of Redbridge*

Keith Gentle, *Senior Inspector for Art and Design, Manchester*

Ron George, *Head of Creative Arts Department, Bretton Hall*

Ernest Goodman, *Ex-Headmaster, Manchester High School of Art*

Arthur Hughes, *School of Art Education, Birmingham Polytechnic*

Howard Jones, *Head of Expressive Arts Department, Rolle College*

Terry Jones, *Drama Adviser, Devon*

Bill Leedham, *Director of Schools Museums Service, Devon*

Shirley Page, *Art Advisory Teacher, Devon*

Raymond Petty, *Senior Lecturer in Art Education, Essex Institute of Higher Education*

Derek Pope, *Assistant Director, Bath Institute of Higher Education*

Neil White, *Art Adviser, London Borough of Hillingdon*

Robert Witkin, *University of Exeter*

I am grateful to the following teachers and colleagues who have allowed me to use documentation or description of their own work in schools within this book:

Marilyn Acs, Colin Bigwood, Christopher Bishop, Alison Brachtvogel, John Broomhead, Paul Cartwright, Robert Chapman, Janet Clarke, Jean Coombe, Richard Dack, Graham Davies, Stephen Disbrey, Richard Dunn, Ian Grainger, David Hamling, Keith Hicks, Robert Hooper, Colin Jacob, Tony Littlewood, Shirley Page, Margaret Payne, Alan Phillips, Tony Preston, Peter Reid, Graham Rich, Anne Richards, Peter Riches, Jackie Ross, Peter Rothwell, Norman Schamforth, Michael Stevenson, Helen Stokes, Vincent Stokes, Peter Thursby, Sara Vernon, Rosaleen Wain, Kate Watkins, Bryan Webb, Neil White, Malcolm Wilkinson and Alma Yea.

I am also grateful to the staff of the following schools in Devon who have allowed me to use the work of their pupils in this book:

Ashburton Primary School, Audley Park School (Torquay), Axminster School, Bideford School, Bridgetown C. of E. Primary School (Totnes), Clyst Vale College, Dawlish School, Eggbuckland School (Plymouth), Elize Hele School (Plympton), Estover School (Plymouth), Exeter College, Exmouth School, Exwick Middle School (Exeter), Great Torrington School, Heathcoat Middle School (Tiverton), Heavitree Middle School (Exeter), Ilfracombe School, Ivybridge School, King Edward VIth School (Totnes), Kingsbridge School, Manor Junior School (Ivybridge), Okehampton School, Paignton College, Park School (Barnstaple), Plymouth High School for Girls, Plymstock School, Priory High School (Exeter), Queen Elizabeth School (Crediton), Sidmouth College, St Margaret's C. of E. Primary School (Torquay), St Thomas High School (Exeter), Tavistock School, Teignmouth High School, Thornbury Primary School (Plymouth), Torquay Girls' Grammar School, Uffculme School, Vincent Thompson High School (Exeter), Whitleigh Junior School (Plymouth), Wilcombe Middle School (Tiverton), Woodfield Junior School (Plymouth) and Woodford Junior School (Plympton).

The authors and publishers would like to thank the copyright holders below for their kind permission to reproduce the following textual material and illustrations:

The Art Institute of Chicago for 'Into the world came a soul called Ida' by Ivan Albright on page 166; the Controller of Her Majesty's Stationery Office for the GCSE National Criteria for Art and Design on pages 251–2 (Crown copyright 1985); Julia McKenzie for 'Vase of tulips' on page 172; The National Gallery, London for 'Hilaire-Germain-Edgar by Degas on page 172.

INTRODUCTION

This book has grown out of my work with teachers as Art Adviser to Devon for the past fifteen years. In that time I have had the privilege of working with many committed and distinguished teachers in both primary and secondary schools, and their work and their thinking has had a significant influence upon my own work as an art educator.

I have tried here to make a bridge between the considerable body of research into the theory of art education that has taken place over the past twenty years and the day-to-day practice of teachers in schools. I hope that my attempts to illustrate general principles with teachers' descriptions of their own practice will help other teachers to measure their practice more effectively.

Although this book is intended mainly for teachers in middle and secondary schools, I have drawn considerably upon evidence of good practice in primary schools to support the text, as I believe that the specialist art teacher can learn much from observing the work of good primary school teachers. For this reason, I hope that this book will also be useful to head teachers in primary schools and to those who have curriculum responsibilities for art and craft in their schools.

All the material in this book is drawn from in-service courses and conferences in my own authority, from working parties of teachers and from observation of teachers working in schools in Devon.

I would also like to acknowledge the very considerable debt I owe to Joslyn Owen, Chief Education Officer to Devon, both for his support and his encouragement over these years and for his challenging ability to reduce an ill-founded theory to tatters.

Robert Clement
June 1985

1 A FRAMEWORK FOR THE SYLLABUS

Art For Whose Sake?

If you discuss the relevance of art teaching with different groups of people within education – or with anyone outside it – you find a perplexing variety of responses. In many schools there is a considerable gap between what the art teacher aims to do – what he/she sees as his or her function within the school – and what the teacher appears to be teaching to other people, not least to the children within their care. Teachers of all subjects grumble about the way that external sources counteract the influences they try to bring to bear within the classroom; the art teacher has also to contend with the whole range of misconceptions about what art is about and what art is not about and should be.

Children's own attitudes towards art, and their understanding of its relevance to them, are only partly influenced by the teaching they receive in schools. Consider this range of views from a group of 15-year-olds who had recently opted to take art for 'O' level. Their attitudes are clearly as influenced by external sources as by the teaching they have received within the art department in their own school.

> Art gives me a rest from the normal school routine.

> Another aim of art which is most important is to get the standard of our painting raised high enough for us to pass our 'O' level examination.

> You can only teach people a certain amount of art – it is mostly talent.

> If a subject had to be dropped in school I think it should be art, because it has no value except to those whose job is on the artistic side.

> I chose art because I like it and don't want to take geography.

> I think that art is valuable because it provides an outlet for self-expression amidst the turmoil of other subjects.

> The value of art in school is that it makes us use imagination and it makes a person use his senses, especially sight – it is a sort of poetry for the eyes.

> I like things neat and interesting. Sometimes I like to break away from this, to feel free, to go mad. This I can express in art. Art is a way of freeing your emotions in a safe way. Art is an outlet.

This range of descriptions by children of how they view their art education matches the curious variety of functions attributed to art in our schools. Traditionally, art departments in secondary schools are saddled with a confusing proliferation of functions, many of them unrealistic and few of them having much to do with children's learning. They are more likely to do with producing certain kinds of images and artefacts, passing on culture, developing good taste, providing a useful therapy for backward children, or a little relaxation from real academic work for the brighter children.

Many art teachers still tend to rely too much upon the products of their work with children as the main justification for the place of art within their school. Although the quality of the children's work is a strong indicator to the strength and purpose of a department, that in itself may not be sufficient. As art educators, we may too easily assume that art making is self-justifying, because we ourselves have spent so much of our lives making art and teaching others to do the same. Many laymen, and many of our colleagues within schools, simply do not share the same faith and need evidence other than the work itself to give support to our convictions.

Within schools, art has to be justified through a description of its value to the learning and development of children. In order to make this justification, you will need to know something of the nature of art as a medium for learning.

Good art education in schools operates within two modes: 'productive' and 'critical'. 'Critical' is used here in the positive sense of appraising and evaluating. The production of images and artefacts is greatly enhanced by informed and relevant experience in the critical role. Although the making of images and artefacts and the critical appraisal of the work of artists and designers is central to a sound education in art, the competencies which good art teaching seeks to develop in children are much more varied and broader in character. Art education in schools also has to take a major responsibility for important aspects of children's development, which is of intellectual, personal and social significance.

Within the schools, the arts do *not* exist simply to provide an affective balance to what is assumed to be a predominantly cognitive curriculum.

It is the case that each of the major cultural forms we call the arts, the sciences, the social studies and the humanities are symbolic systems that humans use in order to know. They are all cognitive. Symbolic systems are the means through which consciousness is articulated and they are also the means through which what has become conscious can be publicly shared.

Eliot Eisner in 'The Impoverished Mind'

Feeling is, of course, important within artistic activity, and art teachers need to help their pupils to refine and sensitize their feelings, but the prior concern within art education has to be with those feelings aroused through aesthetic qualities within the environment and by and through artefacts – with feelings and personal responses related to objective experiences and which are capable of expression through visual means.

The Aims of Art Education

Art education within secondary schools can have a bewildering variety of aims and objectives. They need to be clearly and simply defined, so that they serve as a statement of intent for the work of an art department and provide the logic for the detailed syllabus structure they should support.

Basic aims
There are four general categories of aims, and although there may be overlap between them, there is sufficient differentiation to make them useful as a way of both defining and balancing the work of an art department.

Aesthetic aims are helping children to understand and use the language of aesthetics – and to comprehend the nature and function of art forms within the context of their own work, within an historical context and within the context of their own environment and culture.

Perceptual aims are providing children with the particular perceptual skills needed to comprehend and respond to art and design forms and to the visual environment.

Technical aims are teaching the necessary skills involved in the use and manipulation of materials.

Personal and social aims are improving the quality of children's learning – their abilities to think, perceive, make decisions, work through problems etc., and heightening and improving the children's personal perception of the world and their reactions and responses to it.

Aesthetic and perceptual aims are most important in that they describe those qualities that make art, as a way of learning, unique within the curriculum. Personal and social aims are most important where they are operational – to do with improving and sharpening children's learning. They give weight to the argument that art plays a constructive part in the general education of children. In association with perceptual aims, they play a large part in determining the pattern of work in the first three years of secondary schooling, where it needs to be argued and proved that art provides a useful vehicle for learning and that there are exclusive ways of operating within art that are beneficial to all children, whatever their skills or potential as artists.

Specific aims
On the basis of these four categories of aims, the following might serve as a useful list of aims upon which to base the work of an art department. The aims are to develop:

1 a broad understanding of the meaning, significance and contribution of art, craft and design within both contemporary culture and that of the past;

2 those perceptual skills essential to the construction of visual, spatial and conceptual models of reality;

3 visual literacy – confidence and competence in reading and evaluating visual images;

4 a sense of the quality of visual forms in the environment and of the process of its imaginative recreation;

5 individual expressive powers and the exploration of individual reality through the practical and creative manipulation of visual forms;

6 the ability to hold, articulate and communicate ideas, opinions and feelings about their own work in art and design and that of others;

7 particular individual aptitudes within art, craft and design;

8 skills in the handling of media and understanding of the basic concepts governing the use of different media;

9 a sense of craftsmanship and an appreciation of those skills and efforts required to achieve work of quality.

Example 1 shows how one group of teachers, in the introduction to their syllabus, have considered carefully both the rationale for the work in their department and the way that the aims of the department might be defined by using the categories described above.

A Framework for Art Education

Like all forms of human expression, art (the making of images) is evidence of response to different kinds of experience. Both the experience received and the response that follows can be either objective or subjective.

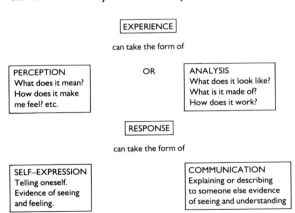

This simple model provides a useful framework for art teachers to use as a monitor of the range of experience they provide for their pupils.

Whatever starting point you use in your work with children, the experience they have and the responses they make will be determined by the context within which you place the event. In Chapter 4, detailed examples are given of the way that children's experience of something as familiar as a house is determined by both the questions asked of the children about the house and the context within which they are asked to view and respond to it. Whether they describe the house, analyse it, tell stories about it or conjecture about it will depend upon how you focus their view of that familiar form.

Similarly, the children's perception of themselves through the making of a self portrait will be determined by the context within which the task is placed, by whether you ask them to describe themselves in as much detail as possible, or to measure themselves very carefully, or to record subtle colour changes in the face, or to make comparisons between themselves looking happy and sad, or to conjecture through the drawing about how they might look in twenty years' time etc.

This is why it is of little use trying to structure an art syllabus on the basis of content or subject matter. You need to consider carefully what kind of *response* is required of the children to each and every task you set them. Example 2 shows how one junior school teacher has used this method to ensure a proper balance of work within her school. Here the teacher considers how to generate a programme of work that is properly balanced between the different kinds of processes and responses that art allows. In your work with children in secondary schools, it is important that you also maintain a balance of work that allows children access to, and experience in, the different modes of working available through the making of images and artefacts. Just as the good teacher of English ensures that children are required to write transactionally, descriptively and expressively in their English lessons, the teacher of art needs to ensure a similar balance within the making of art.

In Example 3, the teachers who designed the project sheets planned the work in such a way as to encourage children working at the zoo to attempt different kinds of tasks and ways of working. They included analysing and recording, comparing and contrasting, communicating and expressing.

The most influential framework or model for art education in schools in recent years has been provided by Maurice Barrett in his publication 'Art Education: A Strategy for Course Design'. In this book, which should be required reading for every art teacher, Maurice Barrett constructs a framework for art teaching which is based upon those three elements within art which are all an essential part of any visual enquiry.

1 The personal or conceptual element creates curiosity and interest in children, places the work within a meaningful context for them and generates feeling responses to the ideas and problems presented by the theme.

2 The technical element is concerned with the organization and use of materials and processes – with the development of skills appropriate to the problem.

3 The visual element embraces perception and understanding of those visual elements that reveal the appearance of the world: colour, tone, surface, line, space, movement etc. It also includes understanding of the different forms of visual response appropriate to the theme or problem.

Any one of these three elements can become the dominant one or the starting point for a particular project – but all three elements need to play their part within the work.

The value of this model is that it enables the art teacher to consider and monitor the balance of experiences presented within a particular project or across the whole art syllabus. Although, in art, there are a multitude of common experiences and disciplines that children should experience and learn, the overriding aim should always be to provide them with those looking, thinking and making skills which will enable them to respond with confidence to their individual and personal view of themselves and their world.

It is particularly crucial to get the right balance between experiences which allow for objective

EXAMPLE I

world in terms of literacy and numeracy, art is a non-discursive mode of knowing. There is a vast area of experience available to us only through the sense of vision. Art is capable of giving shape and form to the ineffable, and there are strong links here with the sensual, mental and emotional life of the individual.

4 Art is directly linked to 'visual culture', and no matter whether this is interpreted as an historical or contemporary link, or both, the fact is that the shape of our world is profoundly affected by our visual culture, and an informed acquaintance with it must be a part of the attributes of anyone counting themselves truly educated.

The above analysis reveals that art contributes to the curriculum in two ways:

1 intrinsic – aesthetic/perceptual, and discriminatory/ appreciative characteristics of the subject, and their attendant implications and offshoots;
2 collaborative – the addition of particular values to the 'learning process', e.g. the characteristic cognitive attributes of creativity, comprising fluency, flexibility, originality and evaluation.

A subject curriculum has to be thought of in relation to the environment in which it will operate, namely the school and the nature of its educational thinking. Curriculum thinking at Kingsbridge is essentially subject-centred, concerned with the transmission and acquisition of subject-specific knowledge and skills, and ultimately directed towards satisfying the demands of the examinations systems. The organization of the school into subject departments, and the types of facilities available, reinforce this philosophy. Other concerns do exist, but they are subordinate and not the focus of the main drive in the working of the school. In order that children will relate effectively to the work of the art department, and profit by it, they must encounter it in a form that is recognizable and understood by them.

In accordance with the above, the art curriculum will be subject-centred in its major orientation, but this is not exclusive of other concerns, such as child-centred considerations, which can be accommodated in later and more detailed stages of design and operation.

Aims   Aims are prescriptive and generalized; they describe the intentions of an educational programme and are prominent in shaping the form and direction of subsequent planning. They thus guard against the all too easy lapse into a dilettante approach lacking in deliberate structure.

Main aim
The provision of appropriate experiences and conditions for learning, within which children may encounter and participate in the modes of thought and feeling actions characteristic of the visual arts.

Sub-aims
An analysis of the intrinsic and collaborative contributions of art to the curriculum yields four categories of aims, from which a range of sub-aims are derived:

1 aesthetic aims – language of aesthetics, nature and functions of art, appreciative dimension;

2 operational aims – thought and perception, quality of learning, discrimination and judgement;

3 personal/social aims – perception of, and response to, the visual world, personal awareness and identity;

4 technical aims – acquisition of necessary and useful skills and techniques, knowledge of tools, materials and procedures.

None of these categories are discreet entities, but exist in a state of interdependence.

Identification of sub-aims:
1 to develop perceptual awareness and sensitivity, and promote the processes of visual discrimination;

2 to develop the ability to appraise and to analyse critically objects, experiences and events in the visual world/environment;

3 to develop the ability to translate an idea/thought/concept into a tangible visible metaphor;

4 to enable children to develop a vehicle through which to advance a personal form of expression.

EXAMPLE 2

EXAMPLE 2

Guidelines for third- and fourth-year juniors

Alison Brachtvogel   *Teacher in charge of art and craft, Whitleigh Junior School, Plymouth*

A framework for an art programme with 9/11-year-olds in a primary school, which has been designed to encourage colleagues to seek for a well balanced pattern of work (see pages 12–13).

Third-year development (9/10-year-olds)

Functions	Skills
Description Continue observational work from a variety of sources, and keep a close link with language work. Encourage looking for own stimulus and keeping a sketchbook. Pay attention to backgrounds now and use different viewpoints, light sources and distortions.	*Drawing/graphics/design* Scale of work – large v. small. Chalk and charcoal. Use of pencil – different grades – explore and develop. Continue building confidence in the use of pastels.
Analysis Look at size and scale – magnify with and without viewfinders. Isolate interesting points and develop. Consider tone and colour.	*Painting/picture building* Building a picture in layers. Use of a wash as a background, small detailed work, small brush work.
Communication Describing actions, conveying feelings, telling stories – look at the work of book illustrators.	*Printing/collage* Repeat patterns – paper and fabric. Collage from rubbings. Mixed media collage. Design specifically for printed work.
Problem solving Problems in conveying 3D image. 3D constructions. Planning for printing using 2 colours or tones. Developing testers, samples, and colour tests.	*3D/textiles* Variety of fabrics and thread – built up work, mixed media, i.e. foil and fabric. Weaving. Paper and card models. Moulded clay work. Rolling and cutting. Building with slabs. Decoration. Finishing and thickness. Group work.
Expression Working from non-visual stimulus – music/poetry. Feelings through colour.	

Third year

	Painting/picture building	Graphics/design	Printing/collage	3D/textiles
DESCRIBING	Industrial landscapes.	Drawing all kinds of machinery and parts. Hand-held – automatic. Hammer and nails. Cheese grater. Pencil sharpener.		
ANALYSIS	Metallic qualities – limited pallette to show rusty, shiny etc.	Working parts – large scale drawings. Clockwork mechanisms.	Foil collage. Mechanical patterns – repeating. Cogs – fitting together.	Pattern in foil and fabric.
COMMUNICATION		Patterns for noises and movements – stop, start, breakdown. Action sequence – opening a tin, hammering a nail.	Print to show movement – push, pull, turn, spin, drag, lift (symbols for these?).	
PROBLEM SOLVING		Design an extra pair of hands. Machine invention.		2D–3D montage – a time machine.
EXPRESSION	Roller skating. The factories take over the countryside.	See also 'Animals and Machines: Movement', a document by Peter Riches of Eggbuckland School.		Clay – industrial landscapes. Industry/machines.

EXAMPLE 2

Fourth-year development (10/11-year-olds)	**Functions**	**Skills**
	Description Continued observational work. Careful choice of media and papers, particularly shape and size. Economy of line, graphic accuracy. Living images. 5-minute sketches.	*Drawing/graphics/design* Drawing for information. Build on previous pencil work. Working in the environment – 'on location', limited time projects. Develop sensitivity in choice of graphic materials – build on confidences, allow choices.
	Analysis Designing for other media – show how some images 'lend' themselves to a particular medium. Changes – metamorphosis and distortion.	*Paint/picture building* Building up expressive work. Observational painting – colour work important. Short painting sketches. Painting with objects other than brushes.
	Communication Analysis of advertising images. Symbols and signs. Feelings.	*Printing/collage* Designing for this purpose. Screen printing. Batik. Tie and dye. Printing for a purpose – tickets, posters. Collage using 2/3 media.
	Problem solving Planning for all work especially 3D constructions. Decision making – group projects.	*3D/textiles* Fabric printing and embroidery. Putting ideas for clay into practice. Large models, figures etc.
	Expression Developing a theme that is not immediately visual – emotions, inner self. Using collected images for imaginative work and building them into a composition. Illustrating literature – poems, fairy tales.	

Fourth year

	Painting/picture building	Graphics/design	Printing/collage	3D/textiles
DESCRIBING	A Medieval Feast (Les Tres Riches Heures), Bruegel's Harvest, Still Life – Cezanne, The Last Supper, A Meal in My House.	Drawing fruit, vegetables, grains.		
ANALYSIS		Enlarge above studies – use as stimulus for printed/textile work.	Printing with hard fruits and vegetables.	
COMMUNICATION	'Butter Mountain'.	Advertising campaign – packets, adverts, magazine, TV (designing set to fit dialogue). Fat v. lean.		Clay 'bad fruits' with worms. Fruit surprises – instead of stones and pips, there is . . .?
PROBLEM SOLVING		Designing new eating/food preparation tools.		Inventing packaging for foods.
EXPRESSION	Fattypuffs and Thinifers.	Design clothing/jumpers for butchers, greengrocers etc.	Food collage – My Favourite Meal.	
				Food.

EXAMPLE 3

CHARACTER task sheet

birds — PARROT / PENGUIN

analyse & record	compare & contrast	communicate & express	resources
draw a parrot and decide which words you would use to describe its character. RECORD the colour.	**choose** a machine which you think is most 'parrot-like' in character.	**incorporate** the chosen machine and the chosen parrot character in a black and white silhouetted form using cut-outs	COLLECT IN THE CLASSROOM:- Pictures of machines with bird names, adverts, incorporating penguins, machinery which might be compared with same.
	look for machines with bird names. Decide what image is being stressed. Find out about the real birds and compare with the image that is put over.	**choose** a bird whose image is light, airy and delicate and make a construction to emphasize this. CHOOSE a bird whose image is strong and powerful and make a study using media to accentuate this.	
observe and draw a penguin. RECORD its markings. DECIDE what sort of character it has 1. On Land 2. In water.	**compare** the image you see of the penguin with the image given it by various advertisers. MATCH your image of the penguin with machinery 1. On land – e.g. R2D2 in dinner jacket 2. In water – e.g. a torpedo.	**design** a pattern in black and white of penguins depicting the character which you have given them.	COLLECT FROM DEVON ZOOLOGY CENTRE:- Books, Skulls, Skins, Skeletons, Slides, Posters. (All items subject to availability).

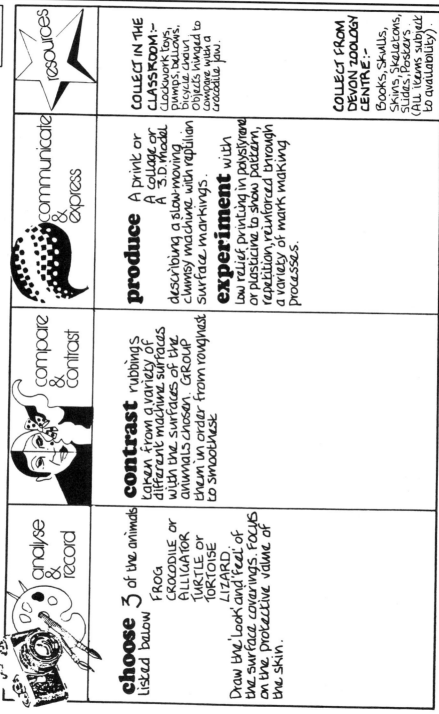

APPEARANCE task sheet

reptiles & amphib

LIZARD
FROG
SNAKE
CROCODILE
TORTOISE

analyse & record

choose 3 of the animals listed below

FROG
CROCODILE or ALLIGATOR
TURTLE or TORTOISE
LIZARD.

Draw the 'look' and 'feel' of the surface coverings. Focus on the protective value of the skin.

compare & contrast

contrast rubbings taken from a variety of different machine surfaces with the surfaces of the animals chosen. Group them in order from roughest to smoothest.

communicate & express

produce A print or A collage or A 3.D. Model

describing a slow-moving clumsy machine with reptilian surface markings.

experiment with low relief printing in polystyrene or plasticine to show pattern, repetition, reinforced through a variety of mark making processes.

resources

COLLECT IN THE CLASSROOM:- Clockwork toys, pumps, bellows, bicycle chain. Objects hinged to compare with a crocodile jaw.

COLLECT FROM DEVON ZOOLOGY CENTRE:-

Books, Skulls, Skins, Skeletons, Slides, Posters. (All items subject to availability).

EXAMPLE 4

EXAMPLE 4

'New and worn' – a first-year project

Jean Coombe   *Head of Expressive Arts Department, Dawlish School*

An art project for 11/12-year-olds in which careful thought is given to the balance between looking, thinking and making skills.

This project is built upon a balance of the three elements that constitute the nature of the art process – the conceptual, the operational and the synthetic. It takes into account the developing characteristics of the pupils involved and contains a sequence of appropriate activities which are rooted in real and direct experience, and which lead to imaginative and expressive response. The use of 'visual source material' is an important feature of the project, as is 'looking and talking' (as a defining, clarifying, reinforcing and questioning etc. agent).

The broad aims of the project are:

1 to give pupils the opportunity to confront their environment through observation, articulation, manipulation, analysis etc., and in so doing build a deeper understanding of it and a firmer relationship with it;

2 to encourage personal statements about the environment, and in so doing liberate and give worth to the feeling response and uniqueness of the individual pupil, so that his/her understanding of himself/herself as a person of worth in that environment is underlined.

'New and worn'   **Session 1**

1 Class discussion based upon the 'worn' parts of various objects – saddle, pipe, spoon, nail, boot. Objects handled freely, spontaneous comments encouraged. A lot of very close investigation – using lenses to magnify and isolate. Various questions inserted to direct the looking and generate specific channels of thought:
     Why do objects change?
     Do they change in the same way?
     Do they change at the same speed?
   Specific references to the objects being handled.

Fig. 1.1 *Photographs used in the initial display to stimulate observation and discussion about the difference between things that are new and those that are worn or decayed.*

2 Drawing activity based upon selected worn object – part or all of it – lenses and viewfinders used to isolate, magnify and to underline the scrutiny required.

3 Session ended with reference to a large board of photographs and words – all related to aspects of worn objects. Emphasis made through matching word (tattered/torn/crumbling/gnarled etc.) and image. Discussion. Homework set – collection of photographs and objects.

Session 2

1 Investigation through looking and class discussion of

EXAMPLE 4

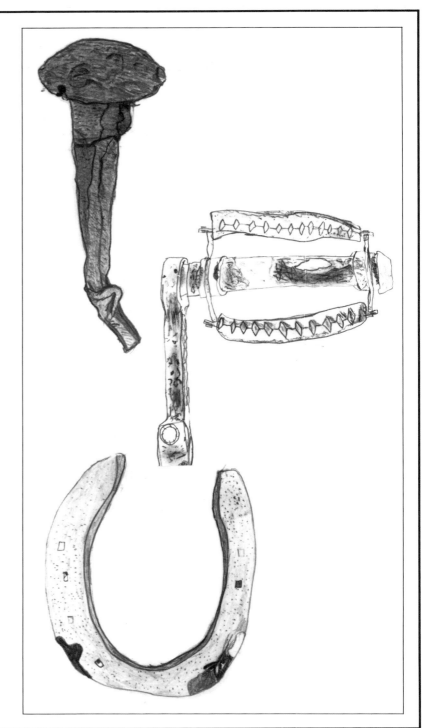

Fig. 1.2   Nail.

Fig. 1.3   Bicycle pedal.

Fig. 1.4   Horse shoe.
Detailed studies in pencil of eroded objects collected by the children. The children were asked to make drawings which described carefully just how and where each of the objects had been most eroded by time or weather.

homework photographs added to the board with words, objects added to the collection.

2 Drawing activity of the previous session continued. Some children now wanting to start again – this time using their own object.

3 Class discussion based upon drawings made and upon old buildings known to the children. Homework set as the previous week, with photographs of old ruined buildings added.

Session 3

1 Discussion of collected homework, with focus particularly upon the photographs of buildings. Reference to a display of photographs showing buildings ruined by various forces.

2 Children asked to select a building photograph from the display (mounted on card), or to use their own, to scrutinize/investigate it – using lenses and viewfinders – to isolate the most interesting part and to draw it. Homework collections continued.

Sessions 4 and 5

Continued drawings with much emphasis upon looking and accuracy. The viewfinders became keyholes or binoculars or windows, through which the observer kept a close watch – becoming an investigator . . . with an eye for detail! Homework – rubbings of various surfaces.

Sessions 6 and 7

Discussion of homework. Locations and quality of marks and patterns. Paint mixing exercise – focus upon secondary and tertiary mixtures, upon different textural qualities and upon old, decaying, worn colours.

Sessions 8, 9 and 10

Paintings – children required to make a painting of an old or crumbling building seen or remembered or invented. Emphasis upon creating an 'atmosphere' of decay.

EXAMPLE 4

Fig. 1.5 Using view finders to make detailed studies from photographs of derelict and ruined buildings. The children were asked to imagine that they were sheltering from a raid or natural disaster and were recording what they could see from their hiding place.

Fig. 1.6 Group colour studies of 'old' colours — working from objects and resources collected by the children.

Fig. 1.7 (top)

Fig. 1.8 (bottom)

Paintings of decaying and ruined buildings — based both upon observation and recollection of environments known to the children.

2 STRUCTURE AND SEQUENCE

Influences upon the Structure of Art Education in Schools

The models of art education discussed in the previous chapter provide guidelines for determining in outline a pattern of art education for use in schools. These guidelines may provide clues as to where your thinking about art education might begin.

Whatever model you choose to underpin your own work, you will need to consider the kind of structure that will make it work and the sequence in which the work will need to take place in order to make it most effective. There are a number of factors that will influence the structure of your work:

1   the changing needs of the children themselves – taking account of their perceptual development and of the shifts and changes that take place in their making and use of images;

2   the organization of the school, both in the detail of its timetabling and in the overall development from a general education for all children towards a core programme plus options;

3   in the organization of the art department, the deployment and use of teachers with different skills and interests and the way that this will influence both the sequence and pattern of work the children experience.

We shall look at each of these in turn.

The Needs of Children

In their years of schooling, between the ages of five and sixteen, children go through three different stages in their perception and understanding of the world. These transitions have a profound influence upon their visual perception of the world and need to be understood in order that teachers can properly match their work to the needs of the children.

Although we are mainly concerned here with the teaching of children in middle and secondary schools, it is useful for the specialist teachers of art to have some knowledge of the route by which the children have passed to them. This is particularly crucial to the planning of work for children in their first year in secondary schooling.

Until the age of six or seven, children are not able to analyse their response to the environment. Their drawing has little reference to formal or traditional forms of visual expression, nor are they confused by the differences between the images they make and those that they see about them. They happily kaleidoscope time, space and scale in one drawing, and it is this very quality that gives the work of young children the vitality and quality of expression that begins to wane as they begin to develop the ability to handle the formal tools of communication. As soon as they are able to convey their thoughts, ideas and feelings through the written and spoken word, the emotive drive to communicate through visual means begins to wind down, simply because it can be satisfied in other ways. At the same time, children begin to develop the ability to see and respond to the world independently of their feelings. They become more objective, more aware of existing visual forms and images and the apparent authority of those forms, and more aware of the complexity of the visual environment and the problem of interpreting the 'real' world. They become more conscious of the differences between the images they make and those that surround them.

The point at which children recognize that the drawings and images they make have public consequences is a crucial one. It is the point at which children begin to compare and relate their drawings both to the real world and to all those other images of the real world that surround them in pictures and photographs, and in film and television.

Between the ages of nine and thirteen, children's image-making is dominated by their need to use drawing, painting and three-dimensional modelling as the means to comprehend better how the world works, how it is put together, what it looks like, how different things compare etc. Through their work in art they can seek better understanding and control of those complex factors that make up the natural and man-made world.

It is here that the teacher needs to begin to support the children's desire to make 'real' images in very positive ways and to provide the source materials, resources, help in looking and focusing that will encourage children to begin to investigate and to communicate through their drawings, as well as to use them as vehicles for personal and imaginative response.

Many secondary school art departments receive children from a large number of primary schools, with considerable variation between schools in the quality of experience the children have been given in this use of visual enquiry to investigate the real world. In many primary schools, and especially those where the work in art is closely linked to work in environmental studies and science, the children may have been given a rich experience in the use of drawing and painting as a means of investigating the real world. In others, the children's work in art may have been almost totally divorced from investigation of the real world and to have consisted of a mixed diet of copying and painting 'imaginative' pictures.

Teachers in secondary schools should have some knowledge and understanding of the work in art in their serving primary schools, otherwise they may not be able to gauge properly the general level of experience the children may bring with them to the secondary school. It does not make any kind of sense for the programme of work in an art department in a secondary school to be based upon the assumption that the children's art education begins here! When at the age of eleven children arrive in their secondary schools, they have already been painting, drawing and making artefacts for the best part of six years. That experience, of whatever kind, has to be built upon and used, otherwise the notion of sequence is totally denied and programmes of work in the first year of secondary schooling may result that considerably underestimate the qualities and understanding that many children may have already achieved through their work in art in the primary schools.

As children approach adolescence, the function of art education becomes more complex. The young adults become increasingly sensitive to their own personal relationships with other people, and to their own social environment. In their early teens, children go through a period of change and adjustment accompanied by all those uncertainties and doubts which can profoundly affect their response to, and use of, images. Frequently, they are no longer satisfied with the making of images that simply describe their experience. They become aware for the first time that an image can express things that have meaning over and above simple description – that real images can have ambiguity of meaning and an emotional context that has personal significance.

This requires the art teachers working with 13/14-year-olds in the secondary school to make adjustments in their teaching. Art teachers frequently refer to the difficulties of teaching third-year pupils in secondary schools and may assume that the problem is only one of social and personal adjustment post-puberty. Just as the good primary school teacher will take account of the 8-year-old's desire to describe the real world, and will adjust the balance of work accordingly away from story telling and towards description, the specialist art teacher in the secondary school needs to re-think the context of the art curriculum in this second stage of transition.

'Please, Miss, I can't draw' is a familiar 8-year-old cry. It doesn't mean that 8-year-olds can't draw; it simply means that the teacher is setting them drawing tasks impossible for 8-year-olds. 8-year-olds are demonstrably very good at drawing simple and interesting things of which they have real and direct experience. When 13/14-year-olds express an equivalent uncertainty – perhaps rather more subtly than the above cry – it is some indication that you may need to re-think the context of some of your work with them.

At the root of the adolescents' uncertainty is a concern to use their imagery to say things that have more personal meaning. This need can be met through some adjustment in the content of your work with them and with more focus upon the various ways that the experiences and skills developed in the first two years in secondary school can be used to support this desire to make images and artefacts that have personal meaning. The various means by which expressive work can be strengthened and supported are dealt with in succeeding chapters.

The Influence of the Organization of the School

The way in which art can be taught to children, and its pattern and sequence, are significantly influenced by the way that schools are organized. The majority of children in this country transfer from primary to secondary school at the age of eleven. In making that transfer they move from one very different kind of school to another.

In their last year in the primary school they will spend at least 75 per cent of their time with one teacher; in their first year in the secondary school they will be taught by at least ten different teachers, and in some schools that operate rotational systems within departments or faculties they may be taught by as many as twenty different teachers in one year. In the majority of primary schools the use of time is fluid; in secondary schools time is tabled in units ranging from 30 minutes to one hour. In primary schools the single teacher of each class allows for much closer links to be established between different areas of the curriculum; in secondary schools these links are much more tenuous, even when art is timetabled in association with other subjects in aesthetic or practical groupings.

As a result, children have to make a considerable adjustment to the way that they learn through art or any other subject. In many primary schools, and especially in those where visual enquiry is a major element of the children's work in environmental studies and science, the children will actually spend a great deal more of their time in drawing, painting and model-making than they can do in the secondary school, where the allocation of time is likely to be between 60 and 90 minutes in each week.

A blindingly obvious question is, 'How do you as an art teacher take account of this in thinking about the work of the first year?'

It is important to know something about the normal pattern of work in art and craft in primary schools, in order that your own syllabus or programme of work begins to make some kind of sense in sequence to what has gone before. Ideally this should be done by visiting at least some of your serving primary schools, to familiarize yourself with the experience the children may bring with them to the secondary school. Where this is difficult, it does help at least to gain some knowledge through detailed discussion with the children, or through the kind of questionnaires shown in Example 1.

The First Three Years

In the majority of schools, art is timetabled as a separate subject for all children throughout the first three years of secondary schooling. There has been some dilution of this principle, especially in those schools where art is organized as part of a general art and design course, and particularly where there have been established rotational systems, carousels or 'circuses' that tend to reduce art to one of the 'materials' areas along-side wood, metal, textiles, cooking etc. (This is discussed at some length in Chapter 7, 'The place of the crafts'.)

In the fourth and fifth years, art becomes an optional subject. It remains a popular option, with between 40 and 45 per cent of children choosing to continue with their work in art, with the majority of those going on to take external examinations. However, this means that for the majority of children in secondary schools, the work of the first three years is the sum total of their art education. We cannot therefore assume that these three years mainly serve the purpose of preliminary training for the more serious work of years four and five. The case for art in the first three years has to rest firmly upon its value to all children.

Within the context of this general three-year course for all children, you have to decide on the skills of looking, perceiving, making and under-standing that are necessary to all children within art and how these complement, strengthen and extend their learning.

A general course in art does not necessarily mean a generalized pattern of activities con-tinuing for three years. The experiences and skills essential to the 11-year-old who has just come up from primary school are very different to those of the awkward adolescent of fourteen. The work of the first three years should consist of a continuous experience in art, where regular and weekly sessions are used to match the de-veloping skills and changing perceptions of chil-dren from the ages of eleven to fourteen. This general course has to be telescoped into 40 sessions a year and about 50 hours of teaching. It has to be taught in week by week units and within larger units of terms and half terms. This requires both an efficient use of time and a real regard for maintaining continuity from week to week, from term to term and from year to year.

Assuming that you have established within your department some kind of model or outline of the overall intentions of your work in art, and that these have been translated into an outline of

aims (as illustrated in the examples at the end of Chapter 1), the next task is to begin to use these to determine the content of your work with children: what needs to be taught, how much of the all too limited time should be spent on each aspect, the order and sequence in which the experiences are best provided.

Example 2 describes how a group of art teachers in neighbouring schools worked to-gether upon the production of guidelines for their work and agreed upon a common pattern across these schools, based upon identifying five areas of experience that need to be included in this core programme for all children:

> observation and recording;
> analytical studies;
> personal expression;
> critical studies and appraisal;
> skills and craftsmanship.

In their planning of these three-year general courses, many art teachers find it useful to use flow charts and diagrams as a means of identifying and giving structure to the pattern of work from year to year. The head of department has to find the right balance between providing enough structure to ensure a comparable experience for all children and allowing individual teachers some room for manoeuvre and the opportunity to make particular use of their own individual skills and interests.

It seems sensible to insist that children should all follow a similar programme of work for at least the first two years. Even with the most generous timetabling, the children will only have about 100 hours of working time in the studios over these two years, and this time will have to be well used to ensure that the children acquire the basic skills of drawing and painting, some experience in at least two craft areas and suf-ficient time for a good supporting programme of discussion and appraisal.

There is a strong case for allowing some variations in year three, on two grounds. The first has already been referred to in noting the changes that take place in children's perceptions of themselves and others as they pass through puberty, and their consequent need to use their image-making more individually and personally. That need can be catered for within the general programme of work, through the gradual introduction of longer working projects within which considerable personal interpretation is both encouraged and allowed. Example 3 describes some half-term projects of this kind, where after some shared work within the two themes 'Time past' and 'Disasters', the children were enabled to explore these ideas in their own terms and in those materials most appropriate to their needs.

The need for a more individual programme of work in the third year also stems from the fact that for the majority of children this is their final year of work in the art department. They do need therefore to have had some opportunity to pursue in greater depth ideas and areas of work that are particularly satisfying to them. The motivation for this may be triggered off by particular ideas, or by certain materials for which they have a particular affinity. Where the work of the first two years is carefully monitored and properly assessed, it should be possible for the art staff to help children identify which aspects of work in the department they could best focus upon during the third year. Where are they most confident, which materials do they most enjoy using, with which resource materials do they find the most affinity, and to what kinds of content do they best relate?

The three-year general course will be fully successful only where it provides both a satisfying and useful experience for all children, and a good grounding for those who wish to pursue further their studies in art.

Fourth- and Fifth-year Courses

The place of specialized courses in art leading to external examinations at 16-plus remains very secure. Art continues to be one of the most popular option subjects outside the core of necessary academic studies. Much of its strength lies in the fact that it offers equal opportunities of achievement to children of very differing abilities. Art does not exclude children who have worthy things to offer but who cannot surmount the often narrow and artificial barriers erected against them in other subjects. Although art teachers are often irritable about the fact that they have to cope with more than their fair share of what their colleagues may define as unmotivated and less able pupils, they can take some comfort from the fact that this is as much a reflection upon the inadequacies of other subject teachers to cope with the normal range of children as it is a description of art as being a dumping ground for the less able. There is no doubt that many art teachers are able to achieve high levels of motivation and response from children who have been conspicuously rejected by other subject teachers. This says a great deal for the value of art education in schools.

What access children have to fourth- and fifth-year courses in art depends upon the option system offered within the school. There is a considerable variety of practice in the design of option systems from school to school. Although the move towards a more common curriculum for all children has resulted in some benefits to art departments, there are still many schools where the option system exists mainly to protect the right of the most able to pursue three sciences or two languages through to sixteen.

Art departments appear to fare better where the art staff have given careful thought to the range of courses that they might offer to children in their fourth and fifth years, and have begun to recognize that the description of 'art' as one generalized kind of activity is not enough to meet the varied needs of 15/16-year-olds.

The pressure upon secondary schools to rethink the kind of curriculum package they might offer to children stems from a very genuine concern that the traditional academic pattern of subject choices does little to meet the needs of something approaching 50 per cent of the schools' population. Art teachers need to respond very positively to the opportunities that are presented through this new realism. Some art departments already offer a limited range of alternative fourth- and fifth-year courses, though these are mainly classified by materials as in pottery, photography and textiles. Other than in very large schools, it may prove difficult to recruit sufficient numbers of children to justify courses as specialized as these.

A more viable arrangement for the average-sized school might be to consider offering courses that are differentiated by the ways of working that are possible within art. By the time they are fifteen, most children – whatever materials they are using – will tend to begin to work in a particular vein. Within painting and drawing, some children will prefer to work very objectively and mainly through direct observation; others will find more satisfaction in making images that are drawn from a variety of sources and that attempt to make complex statements rather than straightforward descriptions. Even within a material craft such as ceramics, where some children want and need to use clay as an extension of drawing and to make artefacts that have personal meaning, others may find greater satisfaction and challenge in the designing and making of useful things.

One art department has successfully dealt with these alternative ways of working by offering three different art courses within the school's option system.

The first, called 'Fine art', is for those children whose interests and skills are centred in painting and drawing, but who may also work three-dimensionally. The course has a strong drawing core and aims to give these children the experiences and skills necessary to use their image-making in a variety of ways.

The second course, called 'Art and craft', is for those who have shown some aptitude across a range of materials and skills and who enjoy making. The course has a drawing and designing core and allows children to specialize progressively in either ceramics, print-making or textiles.

The third course, called 'Graphics', is for those who have shown some aptitude and skills within a narrower framework of drawing and who prefer to use their skills more objectively. The course has a drawing and designing core including layout, presentation and lettering and allows the children to specialize in a variety of graphic design media, including photography.

Example 4 provides useful detail of the way these courses are differentiated.

Where the option system does not allow you to offer a variety of fourth- and fifth-year courses within your art department, it is possible to go some way towards this within the department where fourth- and fifth-year groups are block timetabled together. When two or three fourth-year groups are working at the same time within the department, it makes obvious sense to try to match the different skills and interests of the different art teachers to the needs and interests of the children. In some departments, this is achieved by providing a common programme of work for the first two terms of the fourth year, and by then grouping the children according to their interests with the art teacher who can best match these. Where the programme of work of the first three years has been designed to give the children comparable experiences, so that they enter the fourth year on a roughly equal footing, it is not difficult to plan a common programme of projects for them and to use that experience to assess the kind of course that would then be best for them to follow.

In one school this is managed through the block timetabling of three art groups together. During the first term and a half of the fourth year, all the children work through the same series of four or five project themes, spending an equal amount of time in the painting, graphics and ceramics studios. In consultation with the staff, they then decide which of the three courses available in the three studios they will follow. An important element in the success of this programme is in the design of the projects they follow, the rigorous application of deadlines for completion of work and the group presentation and assessment of the children's work at the end of each project.

Where your department has the advantage of block timetabling, there are a variety of ways in which the early work in the fourth year can be used diagnostically to ensure that children are helped in sorting out the pattern of work that is most appropriate for them.

The organization of children's learning in secondary schools by subject divisions does inevitably lead to argument between teachers, and sometimes conflict, as to how best to share out the precious little time that is available. This is fairly straightforward in the first three years, where there is a general consensus that all children should have much the same spread of experience across a range of subjects. It becomes more complex at the upper end of the school, where subject choice is influenced partly by ability within the subject, partly by the children's liking for the subject and significantly by the children's (and their parents') thinking about future education and work intentions. When at option time art comes onto the open market, the success of a department may depend upon how well its work is understood by colleagues, children and their parents. The more your colleagues and the parents know about the value of art — both its general value to the development and understanding of children and the specific values of the skills and insights it offers — the more likely you are to recruit a genuine cross-section of children to work in the department. Although many of these values are self-evident in the children's work, they can be reinforced through the way the children's work is presented and explained, through exhibitions, through the way in which courses are described and explained in the school's handbook and within option systems etc.

In some schools, the move towards a common core curriculum has resulted in the strengthening of the place of art and craft in fourth- and fifth-year courses, especially where the children are required to maintain study in aesthetic and technical areas through to the age of sixteen. It is important to recognize that art departments can offer courses that have both technical and expressive bias. (See Example 5 for an outline syllabus for a course with a strong technical bias.)

It is important not to be misled into thinking — as has happened in some schools — that the extension of the core curriculum to include aesthetic and practical experiences for all children can be accommodated at the expense of work of some quality and range. Some schools have responded to the movement simply by requiring that children should work in one area within what are sometimes described as 'creative subjects'. As this group can include a range of subjects as disparate as engineering metal work and drama, one choice within this group cannot lead to anything like a balance of experience for the children. At the other extreme there are schools that have established core courses that require children to continue working across a wide range of practical and expressive subjects, but with such a poor allocation of time that the children receive only a minimum of experience in each area and consequently little satisfaction.

It is necessary for art to remain within a core of aesthetic studies for all children until their leaving school. It is equally necessary that children are given opportunities for work in such depth, within their chosen expressive subject, that they have sufficient time and opportunity to acquire the skills and ways of working that enable them to use their art with confidence and meaning. The relationship between art and other subjects within the curriculum is further explored in Chapter 7, 'The place of the crafts', and in Chapter 8, 'Art and other subjects'.

Effective Use of Staff

There has been a general increase in the size of art departments over the past two decades corresponding to the increasing size of schools. Most art departments will now have at least three members of staff, many will be much bigger. Where art departments are grouped in faculties with other subjects, the art staff may well be operating within a unit of up to twenty teachers. This has led to an increasing prevalence in the appointment of specialists within art departments – to teach ceramics, graphic design, textiles etc. The average department today probably consists of four art teachers, at least two of whom will have the responsibility for dealing with one aspect of the department's work. These factors do mean that careful attention has to be given to the way that art teachers with different skills and interests are used within a department, and to ensure that between them they provide a programme of work that makes for some kind of sense and balance for the children.

Within the general art course, all children should receive a basic grounding in drawing and painting together with some access to work in two or three other craft or design areas of work. It is not always enough to assume that a simple rotation of the children between different teachers provides a satisfactory solution to the problem of offering a balanced programme of work, and one that also ensures some sequence of experience from one activity to another. The models of art experience described in Chapter I suggest that a balanced programme of work is more determined by the different modes of enquiry that are possible and essential within art and craft, rather than by the classification of art experience through a division into skills and materials. It is obvious enough that almost any of the materials through which we work with children will allow for a variety of ways of experiencing and responding. The art teacher who works with children mainly through the medium of clay is providing one kind of experience where the making is determined by the acquisition of certain skills, and quite another where clay is regarded as being an ideal medium in which to draw three-dimensionally.

Where children within an art department are being taught by different teachers during the school year, the question of sequence is equally important to that of balance. Especially bearing mind the limited amount of time that children have in their general programme of art and craft teaching, it is more than essential to ensure that as they pass from teacher to teacher, or from year to year, they are given experiences and skills that build one upon the other and which avoid repetition. This places a very real responsibility upon the head of department to ensure that the departmental syllabus serves more purpose than simply providing general guidelines which individual teachers are then allowed to 'interpret' in their own way. This can all too easily lead to needless repetition of skills teaching, exploration of concepts and even of content.

Teachers in different circumstances use various ploys to ensure some balance and continuity within the work of their department or school. Example 6 comes from a middle school for 8/12-year-old children, where art is taught by class teachers. The teacher with responsibility for art has designed these outline programmes of work in each year in order to give her colleagues, who are not art specialists, a clear picture of how skills and concepts might develop from year to year. Careful attention is given, for example, to the gradual build-up and strengthening of skills in different materials areas, and how these relate to the various concepts that children are able to cope with as they progress through the school. Example 7 is a profile used by teachers in a secondary school to monitor the range of teaching ploys and experiences they use from week to week throughout the year. It provides the head of department with a useful and immediate checklist of the range of experiences the children have received in a particular term.

This use by teachers of a variety of teaching ploys in support of their work, combined with giving children access to a range of different kinds of source material, is an important element in providing a balanced programme of work within a department. The use of different teaching strategies and resources within art teaching is examined in greater detail in the next chapter.

EXAMPLE I

EXAMPLE I

First-year questionnaires

Hillingdon Art Curriculum Enquiry 1980
First-year questionnaire used by art teachers in the London
Borough of Hillingdon

Designed by Neil White   *Art Adviser for Hillingdon*

Questionnaire used in St James' High School, Exeter

Christopher Bishop   *Head of Department*

Two questionnaires designed by art teachers to obtain some
picture of the different experiences in art that children have
brought with them to their secondary school (see page 34).

1st year questionnaire

Paper 4

HILLINGDON ART CURRICULUM ENQUIRY

You must not talk to each other whilst answering these questions.
Ask your teacher about anything you don't understand.

1.1 Write the name of your school here ....

1.2 Write your name here ....

1.3 Which class are you in? ....

1.4 Which Junior or Primary School did you go to? ....

Put ticks in the boxes to show what kind of Art you did in your old school.

		A LOT	QUITE A BIT	NOT MUCH	NEVER
2.1 Did you use	Powder paint				
	Ready mixed paint				
	Blocks of paint				
	Big stiff brushes				
	Small soft brushes				
2.2 Did you use	Clay				
	Papier mache				
	Plasticine				
2.3 Did you use	Wood				
	Wood glue				
	Nails				
	Screws				
	Saws				
	Wire				
2.4 Did you use	Old cardboard boxes				
	Old squeezy bottles				
	Cloth				

2.5 Write any other things you used for Art
    and put the ticks in

	A LOT	QUITE A BIT	NOT MUCH	NEVER
....				
....				
....				
....				
....				

3.1 Did you do any printmaking from:-

	A LOT	QUITE A BIT	NOT MUCH	NEVER
potatoes (or other vegetables)				
lino				
screens				
cardboard				

EXAMPLE I

	A LOT	QUITE A BIT	NOT MUCH	NEVER
3.1 (continued) or any other kind of printmaking				
....				
....				
3.2 Did you stick things down to make pictures (collage)?				

4.1 Did you do any special work about

	A LOT	QUITE A BIT	NOT MUCH	NEVER
colour				
patterns				
lines				
tone (light and dark)				
texture (rough and smooth)				

4.2 What other things do you remember doing Special Art work about? Put in the ticks

	A LOT	QUITE A BIT	NOT MUCH	NEVER
....				
....				
....				
....				
....				
....				

	A LOT	QUITE A BIT	NOT MUCH	NEVER
5.1 Did you copy photographs?				
Did you copy other pictures than photographs?				
5.2 Did your teacher tell you what Art to do?				
5.3 Were you able to use your own ideas?				
5.4 Did you do imaginary pictures?				
5.5 Did you look at real things whilst you drew them?				
5.6 Did you go out of your classroom to look at things or places to draw?				
6.1 Did you have a special teacher for Art?				
6.2 Did you have a special room for Art?				
6.3 Did you have a special time for Art?				
7.1 Was your work put up on the walls?				
7.2 Did a teacher mount all the work?				
7.3 Did you mount any work?				
7.4 Did you ever put work on the walls yourself?				
7.5 Did you like the things on the walls in your old school?				
7.6 Did you like doing Art?				

8.1 What did you dislike most about Art in your old school?

_____

8.2 What kind of Art work do you remember doing most of?

_____

8.3 What was the favourite bit of Art you ever did?

_____

8.4 What is the biggest difference you notice about Art in this School?

_____

Thank you very much for filling this in.

EXAMPLE I

1ˢᵗ Year ART QUESTIONNAIRE St. James' High School.

Name .... Tutor Group ....Date.............

Your last school................. Brother/sister in school................

Draw freehand a perfect circle	Draw a can, with front and top.	Draw and Shade a cube.

Name a famous artist ..../.........................
Name somebody you know (adult or child) who you think is good at art ↑

What can you see in this ink blot?

. . . .
. . . .

How many framed pictures do you have at home? ....
What is your favourite and why?. . . . .
. . . .

Do you have any artbooks at home?   Yes/No.
Are you a member of Exeter City Library? Yes/No.

Draw accurately, with details, your thumb →

What do you see in
←this diagram.

. . . .
. . . .
. . . .

Make a list of your hobbies and interests.

. . . .
. . . .

Have you ever been to Exeter Maritime Museum? Yes/No.
Exeter Museum? Yes/No. An art gallery? Yes/No.
Name any other places of interest that you have been to:-
. . . .

Using lettering of
your own choice,
draw a word of
not more than 5
letters in this space →

Tick the space provided if you have used any of the following materials:-
Charcoal ( ) Pastels ( ) Wax crayons ( ) Paint ( ) Clay ( )
Plaster ( ) Pen and Ink ( ) Papier Maché ( )

Tick the space provided if you have tried any of the following techniques:-
Lino printing ( ) Collage ( ) Taken photographs ( ) Colour mixing ( )

In the space below, draw a bicycle, with as much detail as possible.

Complete this drawing in any way that you can think of.

Tick the space provided if you own any of the following equipment:-
Sketchbook ( ) Pencils ( ) Coloured pencils ( ) Felt tips ( )
Paints and brushes ( ) Camera (– what type . . . .)
Any others . . . .
What artwork did you do at your last school? . . . .
. . . .
What is your opinion of it? Circle one letter – Excellent A B C D E – Poor
What artwork would you like to do during the next two years?

. . . .
Art Department Sept. 1983.

45

EXAMPLE 2

EXAMPLE 2

Art in the core curriculum. Guidelines for art education in the Exeter City High Schools

Christopher Bishop   *Head of Art Department, St James' High School*

Paul Cartwright   *Head of Art Department, St Peter's High School*

Marilyn Acs   *Head of Art Department, The Priory High School*

Shirley Page   *Head of Art Department, Exwick Middle School*

Graham Rich   *Art Department, Exeter College*

Anne Richards   *Head of Art Department, Vincent Thompson High School*

Peter Thursby   *Head of Art Department, Exeter College*

Guidelines for art education agreed upon by art teachers from five neighbouring schools which serve the same tertiary college (see pages 34–36).

Although there will be some differences between the City High Schools as to the content of their work in art with first- and second-year pupils, dependent upon resources, staffing strengths and interests, the following areas of experience are acknowledged to be essential to the common course for all pupils in their first two years. These areas are determined by the accepted function of art in these years as a means whereby children are enabled to respond to their environment through observation, analysis and personal expression.

Observation and recording

Much of the work in these two years will be based upon observation and recording from direct experience, in order to encourage careful observation and an understanding of the structure and nature of the world. Through their work in drawing and painting, children will observe and record from a wide variety of source material – both within their environment and from the resource material that is an accepted part of the stimulating atmosphere of a good art room.

The emphasis will be upon recording from first-hand experience. The quality of response and of the children's perceptions will be strengthened by the use of supporting discussion and opportunities to perceive the world through senses other than the visual. In this way they will be helped to realize that the process of 'seeing' is more than the mechanical recording of experiences, and that visual perception requires a combination of intellectual and sensory enquiry. There will be a conscious use of a variety of visual media to support this enquiry and a careful matching of media to task to enable the children to respond effectively, e.g. as in the precise use of graphic media to represent complex and detailed forms, as in the use of colour and tone to represent effects of space and light in nature etc.

Analysis A considerable proportion of the children's working time in art will be devoted to acquiring the basic grammar and vocabulary of the visual world. Children will be taught how to collect and document visual information and how to study and extract from the environment those elements of form, structure, colour, light, tone and surface that determine the appearance of the visual world and our perceptions of it. Some of this work will be based upon direct experience and will take the form of selective recording of the visual elements in the environment; some will be based upon the formal analysis of these elements in their own right, e.g. in the technical exploration of the qualities of one colour, or in the recording of qualities of surface in one part of the environment etc. Much of this work will have significance for the children's understanding of the qualities of design and appearance in the world about them and will relate to and enhance their work in such other curriculum areas as environmental studies, science and design. In addition to the use of a wide range of graphic media, this work will involve the use of a variety of three-dimensional materials (card, clay, wire, plaster, prefabricated forms etc.), especially in the study of those elements of form, structure and surface etc.

Expression In their observed and analytical work, children will be

EXAMPLE 2

encouraged towards an expressive and sensitive response to the world about them, both by the context within which the work is placed and by the use of language (discussion, interaction, writing etc.), in association with their making of images in order to help them to organize ideas and responses to different problems and situations.

They will be set problems and challenges in their drawing, painting and three-dimensional work which will call upon them to extend their imagination within a context that is real and meaningful to them, e.g. in the study of familiar things distorted in different kinds of reflecting surface, or in the making of imaginative analogies for things seen and familiar to them etc.

In class discussion and through the individual dialogue between teacher and child, the children will be encouraged towards assessment and self criticism of their own work at a practical level.

Critical studies and appreciation

In these two years it is considered more appropriate that appreciation of works of art and design should be directly related to and supportive of the children's practical making of images and artefacts. Objects and artefacts will be used to stimulate discussion and enquiry rather than as models or examples of good design or 'taste'.

An understanding of the structure and character of their environment will stem from their drawing and painting from direct experience supported by appropriate discussion.

Much of their work in drawing and painting will be supported by reference to works of art and images in which there is a similar context or in which parallel problems have been explored. For example, colour studies made from a still-life group may lead to discussions about various interpretations of this theme by other artists, where colour has been used selectively to emphasize both formal and emotional qualities within the subject.

The use within art studios of a wide range of source material, both for display and for use (e.g. natural and man-made objects, fine art reproductions, photographs, magazine images etc.) will, implicitly, reinforce within children some understanding of the variety and range of responses that have been present in the work of artists. These may occasionally be more specifically demonstrated by the selective display of children's work in association with both the visual source material from which it grew and examples of the work of artists who have worked on similar themes.

Use will also be made both of practical and of critical work, which will enable the children to have some understanding of the language of the contemporary communications media in film, television and journalism, and of the various ways that images, symbols and language can be used in combination to tell stories, describe events, persuade and exhort. In this area of work, there will be considerable overlap with, and reference to, similar work being done in English and drama departments and the consideration of joint projects where this is appropriate.

Skills and craftsmanship

In all their work, children will be encouraged towards acquiring skills and levels of craftsmanship appropriate to the quality of ideas expressed in their work, and confidence in their handling of media. There will be an emphasis upon using materials both effectively and sensitively and with concern for their qualities, e.g. that a pencil is a subtle drawing instrument capable of producing a wide range of graphic effects and marks, that paint can be used in different densities and applied in a variety of ways, that clay can be rolled, pressed and extended to form different kinds of structures etc.

All children will be given experience of some craft activities, and though these will vary from school to school, depending upon resources, they will include some of the following:

print-making (monotypes, improvised, relief and incised blocks, simple screen printing, etc.);
clay work (modelling, reliefs, simple ceramic structures);
sculpture (constructions in a variety of media, carving and modelling);
graphics (simple typography and layout);
textiles (embroidery and collage, tie and dye, batik, block and resist printing etc.).

EXAMPLE 3

EXAMPLE 3

Two third-year projects

'Time past', Braunton School

Alan Phillips   *Head of Art Department*

'Disasters', Dawlish School

Jean Coombe   *Head of Expressive Arts Department*

Two examples of half-term projects where after some shared work within the themes the children were able to explore these themes in their own terms and in those materials most appropriate to their needs (see page 36).

'Time past'   Third years. Mixed ability. 70 minute modules.

Session 1

1 Introduction to project. Description of how group would work over next few weeks – organization compared with normal working. Some talk about the theme. Group told that the two teachers were going to 'present' a kaleidoscope of their own memories for the first session.

2 Children copied out quotations and verses:

Bergson	*The present contains nothing more than the past and what is found in the effort was already in the cause.*
Sherman	*The best prophet of the future is the past.*
Houssaye	*We must always have old memories and young hopes.*
Johnson	*The true art of memory is the art of attention.*
Nesbit	*All to myself I think of you.* *Think of all the things we used to do.* *Think of the things we used to say.* *Think of each happy, bygone day.* *Sometimes I sigh, and sometimes I smile* *But I keep each olden, golden while* *All to myself.*
Rossetti	*I have a room whereinto no one enters.*

Save I myself alone.
There sits a blessed memory on a
throne.
There my life centres.

Akers   *Backward, turn backward, O time in*
your flight.
Make me a child again just for tonight.

Omar Khayyam   *The bird of time has but a little way to*
flutter – and the bird is on the wing.

Taylor   *A wonderful stream is the river of time,*
As it runs through the realms of tears.
With a faultless rhythm, and a musical
rhyme,
As it blends with the ocean of years.

3   Group given instructions about how they were to use the presentation session the following day. Asked to make notes and doodles in response to readings and records and told that these were to be retained for reference during the run of the project.

Session 2

1   Room set out for presentation with exhibitions of memorabilia brought by the teachers: photographs, books, school reports, objects, a 'special' dress, souvenirs, tickets, programmes etc.

     Tape/slide sequence. Slides of paintings, family photos, places, friends, animals etc.

     Readings and music on tape:
'The Horse's Mouth' – *Joyce Carey*
'The Way We Were' – *Gladys Knight and the Pips*
'Cider with Rosie' – *Laurie Lee*
'As Time Goes By' – *Dody Wilson*
'Preludes' – *T. S. Eliot*
'September In The Rain' – *Tommy Dorsey*
'Portrait of Elmbury' – *John Moore*
'Snowflakes are Dancing' – *Debussy*
'Man and Time' – *J. B. Priestly*
'All Modern Conveniences' – *Clifford T. Ward*

     Children reminded that they were to make any notes and doodles and responses that occurred to them during the playing of the tape/slide sequence.

2   Discussions about sequence – mostly questions from group about souvenirs and memorabilia brought to session by the two teachers.

EXAMPLE 3

Session 3

1 Tape/reading.
   Alternating readings of poetry with music.

R. L. Stevenson	Dark Side of the Moon
Christmas at Sea	*Pink Floyd*
Rossetti Remember	In My Life *Beatles*
Brooke The Great Lover	Tapestry *Carole King*
	Imagine *Lennon*

2 Detailed discussions about the two slide/tape sequences.
   Group given specific instructions about the need for them
   to collect and bring into school things of their own that
   recalled memories of things in the past.

Session 4

1 All children had collected and brought in 'memory'
   starting points for their work – bulk of this was
   photographic. Memorabilia were set out about the room
   and the children – informally – talked to each other about
   things they had collected. Most children toured the two art
   rooms to look at everyone else's collections and to
   exchange information and stories about what had been
   brought in.
      Teachers also engaged with the group informally and,
   where appropriate, encouraged some children into
   recounting occasions in their past.
      Some – a few – children chose which image or moment
   they wished to use as their starting point.
      Music tapes from previous sessions played throughout
   this session.

Remainder of term

Group teaching finished at this point and all work proceeded
on the basis of individual needs and through private
negotiation.
   Group had access to two studios – one for painting and
graphics, one for three-dimensional work and ceramics.
   Project continued for remainder of term depending upon
nature of problem taken up by different children. There was
reference back to the input sessions for about three weeks,
by which time individuals became engrossed in their own
problems. All children found an aspect of their 'time past'
they could use as the basis for their work, and the general
levels of commitment were high throughout the group and
were not just restricted to those with natural abilities.
   The majority of pupils stayed with the image or theme of
their initial choice and pursued this through until they felt

that the images, technically, measured up to the worth of the image, through a progressive refinement.

The bulk of the group worked within the context of realistic images. The work of the remaining 40 per cent was evenly divided between those who used familiar and expressive symbols and those who used combinations of graphic techniques together with written and diagrammatic material.

Disasters

1 Pupils asked to make rubbings of various surfaces around the buildings of the school environment.

Resources
School buildings

2 Discussion of different marks – lines/dots in their various combinations in the rubbings made.

3 Isolation of various parts of the rubbings for drawing. Accuracy and precision emphasized.

Viewfinder lenses

4 Rubble groups set up – each containing one human and personal item – broken toy/photograph/shoe/ necklace etc.

Bricks, broken glass, personal belongings, twisted metal etc.

5 Worksheets distributed showing photographs of old ruined buildings.
Pupils required to make a careful drawing based upon one isolated part.

Photographs

Lenses
Viewfinders

6 Photographs of 'distressed' figures and heads distributed. Discussion of shape, character, mood etc.
Worksheets distributed – pupils required to make studies of various features – isolated facial features/clothes

Photographs

Worksheets

EXAMPLE 3

(folds/creases) . . .
Demonstration of space
shapes – measurement – three
pupils used as models for
figure drawings in poses
representing sadness etc. (as
in photos). Pupils required to
make figure drawings based
on photographs discussed at
the beginning of point 6.

7 Viewing of art work   Art work – Paul Nash
   showing buildings/figures   'We are making a new
   in similar states to those   world'
   focused upon earlier in the   'Monster Field'
   project as well as a   'Void'
   limited colour range.   'Chaos Decoratif' . . .
   Atmosphere and mood related
   to colour.

8 Pupils required to read an   Written report
   account of a hurricane – then
   to make plans –
   drawings/notes connected
   with their responses to it
   (including rubble/figures and
   buildings – not necessarily
   all . . .).

9 Paintings made based on   Other writings and
   selected idea. These took   pupils' work
   four sessions and whilst they
   progressed further stimulus
   was given with readings/
   reports based on other
   disasters involving destruction
   of buildings and loss of life.
   Also as the pupils worked,   Objects
   I was able to build fairly   Photographs
   close contact on a   Art work
   one-to-one basis – talking
   about their work – referring to
   further visual stimulus when
   necessary – as well as to
   discover their own personal
   disasters.

EXAMPLE 4

Upper school examination courses, Great Torrington School

John Broomhead   *Head of Art Department*

A good example of the way that an average-sized art department of three teachers can offer a variety of different courses for fourth- and fifth-year pupils leading to examinations. The outline content of these three courses gives some indication of the different emphasis within each course (see page 37).

EXAMPLE 4

Great Torrington School. Dept. of Art & Design

UPPER SCHOOL EXAMINATION COURSES

DRAWING with FINE ART   OR   GRAPHICS; leading to A.E.B Art/Art & Design or C.S.E.

AUTUMN TERM

F O U R T H — Y E A R

Observed Drawing Assignment:
e.g. Contrast natural with man-made source material.
Comparative use of selected media. Viewpoints/ways of looking.

Introductory Graphic Assignment:
e.g. Introduction to Letter Styles; Ways of producing letters, designs to suit a purpose. Selection & use of suitable media.

Drawing leading to Expressive Work
Develop from personal starting points and/or experiences; Emphasis Used resources e.g. Captions and Captions.

Obs. Select from:
Dwg. i) GRAPHICS
Module   e.g. Package Design.
OR
ii) 2D FINE ART
observed starting points developed from Natural studies Made e.g local environment.

4thYr. Internal Exams

SPRING TERM

Obs.   A. Choose between:
Dwg.   i) Fine Art i) Personal starting point or
Module   ii) Observed starting point.
OR
B. Graphics
choice of two assignments.
Advertising product through poster + sticker or brochure.

GRAPHICS or FINE ART ASSIGNMENT
choice of two based upon Exam 'type' questions and Examiners Reports.

Obs. Dwg. Module

5th Yr. Int. Exams

* (A.E.B. Visual Composition Paper)

SUMMER TERM

EXAMINATIONS

DRAWING with CREATIVE TEXTILES; leading to A.E.B. Art + Design or C.S.E.

AUTUMN TERM

F O U R T H — Y E A R

Drawing. e.g. Tone — Building up Translation of drawing techniques into the Drawing Technique weaving process using diff media. Working from Observation

Weaving based on Previous drawing
Toe.g employing variety of techniques e.g pointillism → tapestry weaving using tufting.

Thematic Approach.
e.g City/Exotic/local landscapes Drawing from photographs and the 'real thing'.
Integrated into Batik (Open ended Approach)

Exploration of other Resist Techniques.

SPRING TERM

F I F T H — Y E A R

Obs.   Exam Based starting point. 5th Yr.
Dwg.   Initially teacher directed to Module provide flexible but positive Int.
Mixed Framework. Choice of diff. Exams textiles media left to student.
(Open ended Approach)

Choice of Exam based Questions + Examiners Report.
(Drawing and preparation translated into appropriate textiles media)

Fine Art Approach using Embroidery Techniques and Printmaking. These as a starting point e.g heads and faces. Initial research through drawing using first & second hand resources.

4th Yr. Internal Exams

SUMMER TERM

EXAMINATIONS

NOTES:

1. Detailed project notes are always required for each module.
2. Emphasis placed upon preparation, use of resources and presentation of completed assignment ready for assessment.
3. Written Assessment Objectives presented to students at the beginning of each assignment.
4. Flexibility between Graphics, Fine Art and Creative Textiles components, especially in fourth yr. This maximises students choice.
5. Homework given on a weekly basis plus relevant holiday projects.
6. All assignments have to be completed by pre-determined deadlines.
7. Each student has a record and assessment sheet to plot progress over the course.
8. Additional drawing sessions are inserted as and when thought necessary. Each drawing session has clearly defined purpose or emphasis Comparative selection of appropriate media and techniques.
9. Main projects are seen as long-term assignments, divided by drawing sessions to re-focus attention of group and allow individuals to 'change gear' for a period of time. Group discussion + individual explanation are important factors of all drawing sessions.
10. Each pupil experiences a module of drawing, creative textiles OR graphics and fine art. They then select two areas one of which must be drawing.
11. Students entering C.S.E. allowed more flexibility between modules.

J. BROOMHEAD 1985.

Great Torrington School Dept. of Art & Design

DESIGN with PICTURE MAKING; leading to C.S.E.

FOURTH YEAR	FIFTH YEAR
Letter Design 1. To identify and select different letter form. 2. To select and control media. 3. To use source material effectively	**Package Design** OR **Picture Making** — Structured projects based on exam starting points, but allowing individual interpretation when desired
Printmaking/Signwriting (Rotation) 1. To control media. 2. To identify and compare different forms of Printmaking. 3. To make a simple print from start to finish.	Module based on Exam Questions: Selection, Planning, Preparation.
Picture Making 1. To develop an idea in sequence. 2. To select and use resources and personal ideas. 3. To work from observation & develop in an inventive/imaginative way.	5th Yr. Internal Examinations. Two Exam Questions. 1. Suitable for GRAPHICS. 2. Suitable for PICTURE MAKING.
3-D-Design/Construction 1. To manipulate materials effectively. 2. To develop 2D notes into 3D form. 3. To produce a 3D piece of work from a given starting point.	Two Exam Questions 1. Suitable for GRAPHICS. 2. Suitable for PICTURE MAKING.
Distorted/Exaggerated Images 1. To select and control media. 2. To work in an inventive/imaginative way. 3. To practice different methods of visually distorting images.	EXAMINATIONS

NOTES:

1. The ability to describe and communicate ideas and plans through drawing is an important facet of each module. This must be distinguished from the more 'formal' academic approach to drawing.
2. Each module has simple, clear objectives which are directly related to assessment objectives.
3. Each student has a record and assessment sheet to plot progress over the course.
4. Each module consists of four weekly teacher directed sessions to provide necessary skill, knowledge and understanding, followed by a two wk. simple assignment related to previous work.
5. Homework is built into the sequence of work of each module.
6. The collection, storage and use of suitable resources is expected throughout the course.
7. All students are provided with:
   i) a plan of the course for the following 12 months.
   ii) a 6 week plan of the work for each module.
8. Detailed project notes are available for each module.
9. Each module should contain an element of language development, both written and oral.
10. Students are told 'what work is expected' by the end of each session. This must be achieved.

J. BROOMHEAD 1985.

LETTER DESIGN — week by week plan.

wk		
1	Examine different letter styles & ways of producing letters. Select 3 contrasting styles of letters. Copy out & enlarge an example of each. Paint in.	Using gouache paint complete. Encourage to change colour, pattern, tone. Emphasis placed upon technique & control of media.
2	Draw out simple name (4-6 letters). Invent simple graphic marks to decorate letter shapes e.g. stripes, circles, borders etc. Colour in, 2 cols per letter, use felt pens.	1 wk assignment requiring students to select a letter style appropriate to a purpose. By way of colour, pattern, tone to develop into eye catching and finished name plate.
3	Using student collection of letter styles: use viewfinder to isolate section of lettering, copy enlarge.	

EXAMPLE 5

EXAMPLE 5

Outline syllabus for City and Guilds Art Foundation Course in vocational art (locally devised), Ilfracombe School

Malcolm Wilkinson   *Head of Department*

A one-year course for children of 16-plus. Designed for students of average ability and who were hoping to progress to further education in art. The course has a strong technical bias within the areas of graphic design and communications and includes work experience (see page 38).

The course

This is a new course, locally devised but based upon the criteria set out by the City and Guilds for certification as a Foundation Course. It covers a wide range of occupational interests under a broad based vocational heading and is designed to satisfy the concepts and ideals of a C & G Foundation Course and the demands and expectations of both students and employers in the area.

The course provides an opportunity for the student to study, research and experience the wide field covered by vocational art. Whilst catering for the largest possible areas of extension of employment in the area, the width of study allows the greatest chance for transferability of skills. The inclusion of a wide choice of additional studies (GCE/CSE) enables either the reinforcement of an interest or the diversification of qualifications. This will give the student the added advantage of widening his sights to include further education or training, by allowing him another chance to gain the qualifications needed for entry.

Negotiation and integration

The setting up of the course has taken into account the maximum use of negotiation opportunities. The students will discuss the training areas relevant to their potential and interest, in order to agree a programme suitable for each individual. This bias will be picked up in the vocational, core and additional studies work.

The integration of the whole course is seen as fundamental, and the maximum use of the work experience, simulated and real, will be used in many of the other areas. The communication studies, guidance and environmental studies sessions will act as a focal point to draw all the aspects of the course together.

Skills and practices

To save repetition, these two areas covering the skills area of the course will be taken together. Many areas of the syllabus covered by these headings cannot be split, as many of the wider aspects of art can only be covered by experiential learning.

Two-dimensional art and design

Consider and develop the various methods of drawing for:
(a) the gathering of information;
(b) expression;
(c) communication.
Be able to prepare accurate working drawings. Consider the use of drawing as:

(a) a diagram;   (d) a caricature;
(b) a symbol;   (e) a plan;
(c) a cartoon;   (f) a map.

To be able to understand and use the basic colour wheel, pattern making, shape and texture. To understand the effect colour, texture and shape have on the ambiance in nature, architecture, advertising, fashion and interior design.

Three-dimensional art and design

The exploration and appreciation of shape, structure and form in both natural and man-made environments. The conveyance of ideas and observations from the above using the various materials available. The examination and appreciation of light and coloured light forms.

Graphic and reprographic design

To consider and appreciate the possibilities and limitations of various reprographic methods and machines. To look at lay-out, paste-up and mounting as a form of presentation. To appreciate the different forms of paper, card, glue, ink and pencil available. The development of lettering/sign writing skills by using:
(a) lettering pen;
(b) brush;
(c) Letraset;
(d) stencil.
To demonstrate the ability to design a logo or symbol for industrial or commercial purposes. To design and produce graphic packages, e.g.
(a) theatre sets, posters, tickets;
(b) letter headings, envelopes, business cards.

EXAMPLE 5

Photography

To understand and develop the necessary techniques and skills needed to take black and white photographs and to make a print from the negative using an enlarger. To examine the various possibilities of linking photography with:

(a) presentation;

(b) graphics;

(c) screen printing.

Gathering information needed for further work with the camera. Show knowledge of the workings of single lens reflex and twin lens reflex cameras.

Office/studio practice

The costing of materials and labour involved in production. The preparation of simple accounts and invoices paying attention to profit percentages and VAT. The costing of machinery; its value and depreciation.

EXAMPLE 6

Extracts from guidelines for art, Exwick Middle School, Exeter (8–12 years)

Shirley Page *Art Advisory Teacher, Devon*
Ex-Head of Art Department, Exwick Middle School

Guidelines for art and craft in a middle school for 8/12-year-olds. Art is taught by class teachers in years 1 and 2, and these guidelines were designed to help non-specialist teachers understand how skills and concepts might be developed and built upon from year to year (see page 39).

THE CHARTS

The following charts may be used in one of two ways. As an individual check list for each child so that his progress through the school is mapped on a personal basis or as a class chart showing what has been accomplished in each year with each group plus an attached list specifying what each child chose and completed for the individual project.

The charts are intended, as a guide only, to show what it may be possible to do, whilst avoiding any intention to treat this as a linear subject, it will show some progression in the work over the four years and avoid repetition. It should also be possible, in the knowledge of what has gone before, to ensure the most varied programme of experience with the minimum of paper work. No detailed list of subjects is given as this is already extensively covered in other publications - see Schools Council Papers. Art 7-11, Devon County Publications and many others. In addition each teacher will have his own ideas about actual subjects. This guide strives only to show what may be appropriate to each age group and to monitor progress.

Time allowed for Art should be half a day a week. Less than this will not allow the right attitudes to develop, those of enquiry and exploration, without pressure. A division of the work spread over the year should be in the order of half spent on drawing and painting, a quarter on the one craft chosen and a quarter on the individual project.

EXAMPLE 6

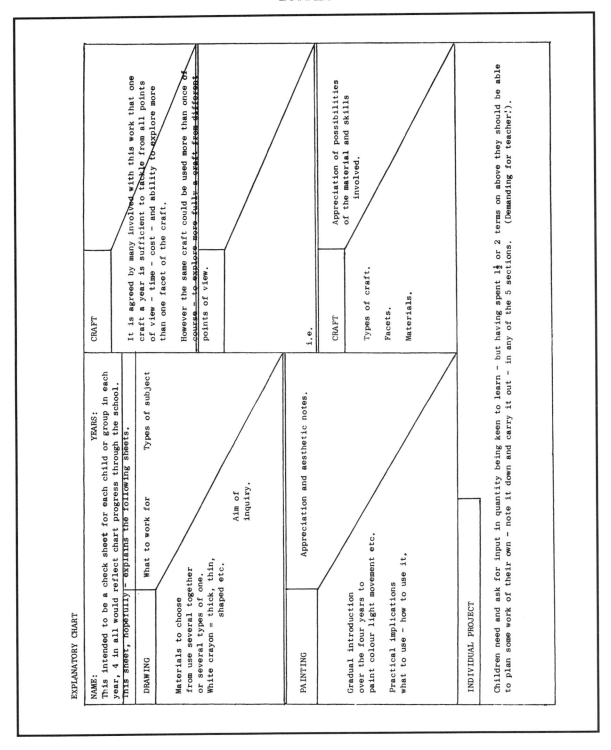

EXPLANATORY CHART

NAME:
YEARS:

This intended to be a check sheet for each child or group in each year, 4 in all would reflect chart progress through the school. This sheet, hopefully, explains the following sheets.

DRAWING — What to work for — Types of subject

Materials to choose
from use several together
or several types of one.
White crayon = thick, thin,
shaped etc.

Aim of
inquiry.

PAINTING — Appreciation and aesthetic notes.

Gradual introduction
over the four years to
paint colour light movement etc.

Practical implications
what to use - how to use it.

INDIVIDUAL PROJECT

Children need and ask for input in quantity being keen to learn - but having spent 1½ or 2 terms on above they should be able to plan some work of their own - note it down and carry it out - in any of the 5 sections. (Demanding for teacher!).

CRAFT

It is agreed by many involved with this work that one craft a year is sufficient to tackle from all points of view - time - cost - and ability to explore more than one facet of the craft.

However the same craft could be used more than once of course - to explore more fully a craft from different points of view.

i.e.

CRAFT

Types of craft.

Facets.

Materials.

Appreciation of possibilities
of the material and skills
involved.

NAME OR GROUP	1st YEAR	PRINTING	
DRAWING	Expressive subjective work. Imaginative work using the environment. (Praise and approve to give confidence). Child centred work. Map of your town or village, school, animals, birds, pets, family.	**PRINTING**	Picture-prints. Simple repeats. Use of dyes for fabrics. How to handle printing inks.
Large pencils. Wax crayons. Large variety of coloured sugar paper. Chalk.		Potato prints. Finger prints. Direct litho (drawing on a glass screen for monoprints.) Flour paste batiks and block prints on fabric.	
		CLAY	Feel for the plastic quality of the material. Outline of possibilities ie. pottery modelling etc. Brief description of firing process.
		Fingers. Rolling. Squeezing. Pinching.	Tiles with incised and relief decoration. Slab modelling. Time to play and experiment.
PAINTING	(Encourage awareness and self confidence) Patterns – natural and man-made. Selecting colours. Simple mixing. Expressive child centred subjects from their daily life and experience.	**3D**	Introduction to sculpture. Feeling for using space. Filling an area. Influence of colour on form. Light and shade.
Large brushes. Tub colours. Powder colours. Felt tip pens (large). Coloured inks.		Junk constructions. Simple models of animals etc., in folded card. Simple mobiles. Diorama (cardboard boxes).	
INDIVIDUAL PROJECT			
Expressive subjects which have a basis in their own experience and whole to consist of drawings, paintings, descriptive writing, poems.			

EXAMPLE 6

NAME OR GROUP   2nd YEAR

DRAWING

How much information is conveyed about the subject.

Imaginative and expressive subjects.

"How things work". Pictures.

Pencils.

Brush and one colour.

Black felt tip (or one colour).

Chalks.

Aim to see the different effects and qualities produced in biro and white paper/chalk and black etc. scale of work.

PAINTING

Illustration. Use of pictures with writing and to illustrate and be part of project work.

Paintings of experiences holidays, sports, circus, seaside etc.

Brushes fine and large.

Block paint. Powder paint.

Collage coloured papers and fabrics.

Picture-making with coloured tissues.

PRINTING

Pictures.
Repeats.
Build up paint in colour and draw with black ink (forest etc.)

String, objet trouvie.
Sponges.

Cut and torn paper.

Cut-out card making raised surface.
Wallpapers for texture.

CLAY

Demonstrate ability of clay to be used as building material in making models piece by piece.
Illustrate with chinese models and English pier groups

Group work.
Simple building with blocks and coils using slip.

Cut out slab figures.

Rolling out and pressing into home made paper moulds.

3D

Group work gives an understanding of the growth of a model as it exists and co-operation and planning in the making of it. Individually keep models small and simple.

Group work.

All materials used to be transformed by paint or surface treatment and built with a larger construction. (Farm, fire station, etc.) Mobiles - different forms on common theme.

INDIVIDUAL PROJECT

Choose a subject and collect all items to illustrate this. (ie. leaf, branch, seeds, flowers of one tree). Write about it, draw it, paint and reproduce in any form which is relevant to what has been covered in the year.

NAME OR GROUP	3rd YEAR

DRAWING

Information collecting and analysing. How to choose what to use from sketches for a painting. Observation. Communication work. How do I get to school. How do things grow.

Pencil - soft - hard.
Charcoal and chalk.
Brush and two colours.
Pen and ink.
Black biro and black felt tip.

PRINTING

Find new things to use and experiment. Analyse natural forms and use as basis for design.

String.
Straw and seed blocks with glue.
First stage screen print with torn paper. Polyprint blocks.

CLAY

Concentrate on form of work as model or pot being well finished, of even thickness and well made.

Pressed moulds.
Hump moulds and pebbles.
Rolling out and cutting.
Decorating with slip. Burnishing.
Incised and pressed pattern.

3D WORK

Spatial relationships area. Containing shapes within a given space. Pre-determined choice of size and colours limited.

Any cardboard boxes, used containers.
Glue, string, polystyrene etc. Individual construction of model or mobile.

PAINTING

Colour mixing Primaries, Secondaries, Tones, Tints, Types of paint. Illustration. Stories and poems.

Brushes.
Use of all sizes wash to detail.
Blob and blow.
Ink blot.
Paintings developed from ideas recorded on out of classroom visits.
Relationships - large figures - drawing and painting each other.

INDIVIDUAL PROJECT   **TERM/YEAR**

Making things. With an aim in view - (play, project, or theme) - draw and paint relevant objects. Try to show how this can be interpreted as a little display of work involving as many skills and methods (points of view) as you can.

EXAMPLE 6

NAME OR GROUP   4th YEAR

DRAWING

Pencil - very soft to hard.
Charcoal and chalk.
Brush and paint.
Ink.
Biro. Felt tip.
Viewfinder.
Magnifying glass.
Reflecting surface
Mirror.

For information. From life. " objects. Use of environment. Houses, building sites. Draw as a preparation for all craft work.
Texture.
Shape.
Line.
Development of pattern from nature and mathematics. Inquiry into scale and size and their spatial effect. Enlargement and distortion.
Structure of living plants etc. Perception. Selection.

PAINTING

Poster colour. Powder paint.
Blocks.
Use of medium with powder colour.
Distance.
Space.
Nature and effects of tone in colour and neutrals.
Making tones and tints from one colour (sheet of blacks or reds).
Use of variety of materials (inc. collage) for imaginative expression.

Apprec. of 2D form space light movement and how to colour select for paintings.
Looking at paintings for qualities (gallery if poss.). Individual and group. Discussion.
Texture.
Shape.
Line.
Colour.
Pattern.
Colour mixing.

PRINTING

Paper print.
Block.
Lino prints.
Screen prints.
Fabric. Batik. Tie and Dye. Block

Appreciation of texture, form and line. Feeling for types of print and ink. Advertising images. Landscape.

CLAY

Models. Pots. Slab, Thumb, Coil.
Relief inc. Tiles.
Slip trailing and incised slip work.
Glazing and decoration.

Feel for material. Appreciation of finer work. Working with a model. Texture and pattern to fit shape etc.

3D WORK

Card and straws.
Wire.
Wood. Modelling.
Metal. Carving.
Plaster.
Junk sculpture (ie. space ship).

Apprec. of space. Construction made from limited number of items. Enamelling.

INDIVIDUAL PROJECT FOR THE YEAR

Thematic approach. Choose some object or group to study record information (collection of drawing) analyse and synthesize.
Choose area to work in - paint, clay, print, 3D, develop ideas and translate into work in chosen form.

EXAMPLE 7

Project profiles, Great Torrington School

John Broomhead   *Head of Art Department*

A profile used by teachers in this department to monitor the range of teachings, ploys and experiences they use from week to week and project to project (see page 39).

EXAMPLE 7

Great Torrington School
Art Dept. - Project Profile.
Teacher.................Yr........
Project.............................

	Week 1	Week 2	Week 3	Week 4	Week 5	Week 6	Week 7	Week 8	Week 9	Week 10	Week 11	Week 12	Week 13	Week 14	Week 15	Week 16	Week 17	Week 18	Week 19	Week 20
1. analytical thinking																				
2. use of formal elements (line, tone, colour.....)																				
3. practical skills/techniques																				
4. problem solving																				
5. use of photographic resource.																				
6. use of direct resource																				
7. drawing in response to sensory perceptions																				
8. drawing from observation																				
9. Teacher demonstration																				
10. awareness of art forms (past and present)																				
11. group interaction																				
12. other.........																				

3 TEACHING STRATEGIES AND RESOURCES

Strategies and Resources

As an art teacher, like any other teacher, you have available to you a variety of systems and resources that you can use in support of your work. The interplay between teaching systems and support material plays a very important part in determining both the quality of experience you provide for your children and the nature of their response.

Reference has already been made to the need to provide for children a rich variety of visual and personal experience in support of their programme of work in art. The art teacher who fills his room with interesting collections of natural and man-made things, good photographs and reproductions of works of art, and who directs the children's attention towards the environment that surrounds the school, is more than half way towards ensuring that the children have sufficient to feed the mind's eye.

Such basic visual provision as this can be made even more effective when the visual experiences are well matched to the variety of strategies that you can use to focus children's attention and to generate the quality of discourse and enquiry that is the hallmark of the really effective teacher.

Here is a list of the various teaching systems and resources that, when used in different combinations, will provide you with a variety of strategies in support of your work.

The use and allocation of time is an important supporting element to all these systems.

Talk and Interaction

By far the most important system any teacher can use is that of generating enquiry through talk,

Systems	Resources
Telling them (exposition)	Images
Questioning (teacher-based)	Natural things
	Man-made things
Discussion (teacher/child)	The environment
	Places
Interaction (between children)	Events
	People
Enquiry (child-based)	The school
Tasks	Children
Writing – copying	Words
note-taking	Sounds
information	Music
collecting	Prose
Resource collecting	Poetry
Worksheets	Children's work
Questionnaires	Works of art
Doodling	Artists
Mark-making	Exhibitions
Image-collecting	etc.
Image-making	
etc.	

whether through exposition, questioning, discussion or interaction. There is no doubt that there is a strong correlation between the quality of children's work in art and the amount and quality of discourse that both precedes and supports the work. There is very clear evidence for this, especially in the work that is done in many primary schools, where good class teachers who have had very little experience or training in art are able to generate work of considerable quality simply through their ability to focus children's observation and perception through good talk in support of their looking.

The pressure of time upon the typical secondary school curriculum, and especially the division into 35- or 40-minute modules, does discourage some art teachers from making sufficient use of talk and appraisal in support of their work – a feeling perhaps that the children aren't working unless they are drawing or painting or making something! I have witnessed many art lessons where the teacher has used only a brief exposition to start the lesson and has relied entirely on individual tuition to maintain the children's enquiry. Other than when working with small groups of well motivated and older children, this is a very limited system of teaching and one that is ill suited to motivating and directing a group of 30 children, who may be with you for only an hour or so.

Instruction or exposition or 'telling them' has its place, especially in relation to demonstrating basic techniques or skills, or in simply setting out the map of the lesson. It always needs to be reinforced through questioning to make sure that what has been stated has been understood by the majority of the children in the group.

The use of questioning in association with looking is one of the most important and basic methods of teaching available to the art teacher. Children see as much through talk as they do through direct observation, and especially in a society where they spend a great deal of time viewing or scanning television (a very passive form of looking). A good teacher can help children to see more perceptively through good questioning and talk, and through this means can give them new perceptions of even the most mundane and familiar things. The use of talk, and especially questioning, in support of drawing is dealt with in some detail in Chapter 4, 'Teaching drawing'.

In some circumstances it makes sense to use questionnaires in association with looking, especially where the children are to work from their own individual source material and where you wish to retain the information and response over a longer period of time. Good questionnaires can be found in Examples 2 and 3 at the end of Chapter 4. They use skilled and detailed questioning to encourage children to look carefully at their shoes and themselves respectively.

Questioning and questionnaires may be used for sharp focus upon particular detail of content. They can also be used more open-endedly to encourage surmise or speculation, as in the questionnaire which accompanies Example 1 at the end of this chapter. This project plan is usefully divided into three sections: teacher activity, pupil activity and resources/materials. Note the variety of teaching ploys and methods used in this project, which include exposition, questioning, filling in questionnaires, class discussion, group discussion, group collecting, interaction and role play, working in small groups, in pairs and individually.

This deliberate use of sub-groups and pairs of children is a most useful way to avoid questioning and discussion becoming too much dominated by the teacher or, as frequently happens, by the few most articulate children in the group. Also, children will respond much more confidently to an open class discussion when they have had the opportunity to share their observations and views within a smaller group first. This is particularly true of any attempt to generate appraisal by the children of their own work or of the work of others, where they are frequently inhibited by being asked to make general comment to the whole class.

It makes similar sense to use a variety of group sizes within the class for any work that is essential, and preliminary work to the making of individual images. The work can be in the form of note-taking, collecting information, collecting resources, making experiments etc. as in any of the following:

writing down words which describe the object to be drawn;
comparing orally two or three very similar things;
collecting useful visual information or reference

material from books or magazines;
making and mixing particular colours;
experimenting with materials to discover a
range of tone, surface or pattern;
observing visual phenomena;
etc.

Sharing this kind of work in groups makes better use of the time available than to require each individual child to repeat the same programme of work. Children can learn a great deal from each other, and their understanding of concepts is certainly strengthened when they work together in this way. Children will, for example, learn a great deal more about colour if they explore certain qualities of mixing and matching in small groups, rather than if they are each expected to make their own individual colour wheel or chart. Children also learn a great deal about visual phenomena through observing and talking about them, as well as by recording them in drawing and painting. When, for example, you embark upon a project dealing with one of those basic and essential concepts to do with colour, or perception of light, or the exploration of surface, it will help key the children into the concept if they are first asked to investigate the phenomenon through a combination of observation, talk and interaction.

Section 2 of Example 2 describes some initial activities that might usefully precede the more traditional means of observing and recording aspects of light and dark. This project, which can be used as the basis for anything up to a term's programme of work, has been designed to make full use of the variety of strategies and resources that can best strengthen and support children's understanding and use of the phenomenon of light.

Workcards and Project Sheets

In some circumstances it is helpful to use work-cards, or individual project sheets, in support of your work with children. These are useful where you need to provide technical information in

support of a project, and where the workcard might provide that basic instruction to undertake a simple task. Example 3 is of this kind of information sheet – they were designed to be used in support of a project on 'Reflections'.

Worksheets are almost essential whenever you embark upon work where the children are likely to be widely scattered outside the studio. In these circumstances, it is very difficult to provide that individual tutorial support that is possible within the art room, and the children do need that detailed reminder of what they are seeking in the environment to encourage them in their studies. A simple instruction sheet can be used to help and remind children of the task in hand.

Worksheets may also be used to set the children fairly basic tasks, such as those included in Example 4 at the end of Chapter 4. These graphic communication worksheets work well because they set the children a manageable task and provide enough clues for the children to pursue the idea without constant support. Worksheets can also be used to cope with the different speeds at which children work within the art room. In almost any project that you undertake with your children, you will find a proportion of the class finishing their task competently and well in advance of many of their fellow pupils. It is much more constructive to give those children who finish first additional tasks to work upon – such as those outlined in these worksheets – rather than to rush the slower workers towards an unsatisfactory conclusion, or to make them leave their work unfinished in order to keep pace with the others. The child who goes through a whole term without being given time to finish the bulk of his work is bound to feel frustration and dissatisfaction at his efforts.

Worksheets can be more complex, such as those in Example 4 at the end of this chapter, which were designed to be used by teachers as part of a long project on the exploration of different kinds of space. These worksheets map out the various ways in which the contrast between things that are large and small might be explored with children, and they provide information about the different tasks that might be pursued and those resources that might best support the work.

Time, Scale and Tasks

The structuring and use of time is an important element in the teaching of art. Even allowing for the fact that children do work at very different speeds, there are occasions when you need to set specific time allocations for different kinds of work. This is particularly true of all that work that may be described as preliminary investigation. Examples 1 and 2 both illustrate the way that a particular lesson may be subdivided with time allocated to such different activities as class discussion, group discussion, note-taking, material exploration, observation of source material, interaction, making images etc.

Children respond well to being given clear guidance as to how much time they have for a particular task, and they enjoy the challenge, for example, of making six different kinds of drawing in one hour, or – in small groups – seeing how many colours they can make with three different colours in the space of fifteen minutes.

Almost anything you choose to ask the children to draw or paint is worthy of some kind of preliminary investigation. Even a pencil drawing of a simple object is best preceded by, say, five minutes of work in pairs to find ten words to describe it, five minutes to see how many different shades you can make with the pencil, five minutes to practise drawing the shape, and then half an hour to make the drawing. The more complex the task, the more detailed needs to be the preliminary investigation.

Figures 3.1 and 3.2 illustrate the work from a class of 12-year-olds working on a theme of metamorphosis. In this project the time was allocated as follows:

15 minutes to practise the range of tone possible to achieve with 2B, 3B and 4B pencils;
20 minutes' talk about their own shoes;
30 minutes of practice drawings;

Fig. 3.1 Shoe drawings; pencil (24 × 20cm).

Fig. 3.2 Metamorphosis of shoes into landscape; coloured pencils (34 × 27cm).

These objective drawings of their own shoes were used by these children as the basis for a project on metamorphosis, where they were asked to change their shoe into a landscape or building. A good example of using objective drawing as the starting point for an expressive piece of work. 12-year olds, Heathcoat Middle School, Tiverton.

72

5 minutes' evaluation;

90 minutes to make careful shoe drawing;

15 minutes to make a tracing from original drawing;

30 minutes' discussion about how their shoes might change . . . into what kind of landscape or buildings;

30 minutes (homework) to make preliminary studies for metamorphosis;

20 minutes' evaluation of studies;

30 minutes practising colour mixing and shading with coloured pencils;

120 minutes to make the shoe/landscape drawings.

Figures 3.3–3.7 illustrate work from a group of 15-year-olds who were investigating the possi-

bilities present within the idea of 'The landscape in me'. These children had the advantage of working together for four days, on an end-of-year project. They spent the first two days (approximately ten hours) investigating the idea through discussion, looking at the work of other artists, writing, collecting information about landscapes and people from magazines and other sources, making preliminary studies of themselves and other people, constructing and lighting artificial landscapes using materials and found objects etc. They then used the last two days to make a painting/collage or construction of a landscape that had qualities they recognized in themselves or in other people. In their different ways, both these projects reflect the importance of using time constructively and of investing time

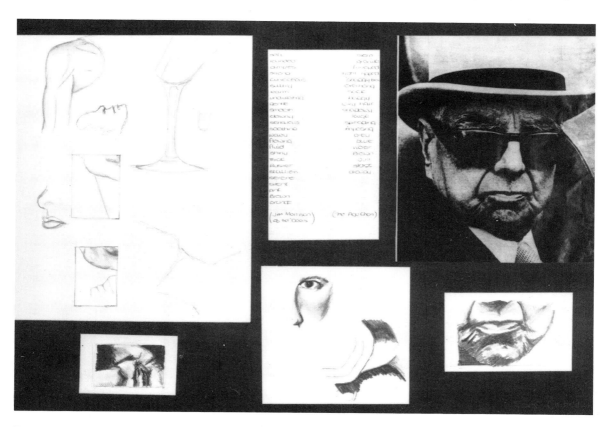

Fig. 3.3   Study sheet; mixed media (82 × 56cm).

in the variety of tasks and investigations that best support the work.

There are of course enormous advantages in trying to find within the school year such concentrated periods of working time as described in the last project, especially with older children. In some authorities, this can be achieved through using residential centres – where a school can book in a group of children for up to a week at a time. In others, it is possible to organize local workshops for children from several schools when, especially during the latter part of the summer term, it is possible to give children an opportunity for an intensive period of work in art without too much disruption to the normal school curriculum. Many children find the challenge of having to work in this kind of way most rewarding. The demands of having to pursue a particular idea or theme for several days does give them some notion of what it is like to study art in further or higher education, in addition to the advantage of being able to work uninterrupted by that wretched bell!

Work by children at Dawlish School who spent four days investigating the relationship between people and landscape. The preliminary work involved making studies of themselves and other people and collecting information about how other artists have painted landscapes in a very personal way. They went on to make paintings/collage of landscapes that had qualities they recognized in themselves and in other people. Three 'personal' landscapes resulted from this project – illustrating the way that these children had been enabled to make individual interpretations of landscape through this kind of investigation.

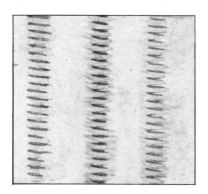

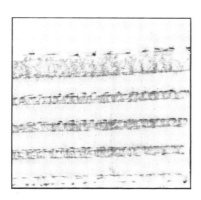

Fig. 3.4   Study sheet; pencils and rubbings (20 × 24cm).

Fig. 3.5   Painting/collage (80 × 60cm).

Fig. 3.6 Mixed media
(75 × 52cm).

Fig. 3.7 Water-colour and
inks (60 × 38cm).

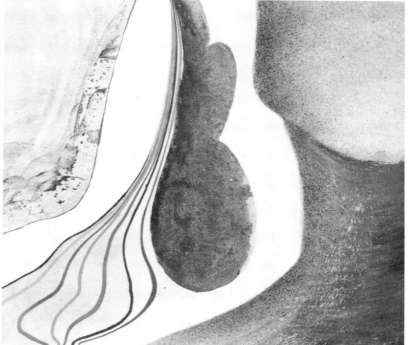

Figures 3.8–3.10 illustrate some of the work done by 15-year-olds in the East Devon area who attended a four-day workshop at the end of the summer term, when they spent the first two days working and making studies in various parts of the Royal Devon and Exeter Hospital before going on to develop these studies further in the studios at Exeter College of Art and Design.

When at the beginning of the fourth year, children embark upon their two-year course leading towards an examination at 16-plus, it is necessary to give them some kind of preview of what the two-year course entails – how they might use their time and what alternative projects and kinds of work they need to cover. It is not enough to assume that now they have 'chosen' to do art the children are able to determine their own individual programmes of work. Although a minority may well have the ability and motivation to do this, the bulk of children still need some kind of structure to work to. Many heads of department have found it useful to provide an over-view of the two years' work by giving the children an outline or summary of those areas of work that have to be covered, what alternatives exist within the syllabus and what the deadlines are for completion of certain projects. Example 5 usefully spells out to the children in the school how they should use their homework and free study time over five terms, in order to strengthen their basic drawing skills across a range of different kinds of source material.

The variety of strategies you use in your teaching will make a considerable difference to the kind of response you receive from your children in the art room. It is all too easy for art teaching, or any teaching for that matter, to become predictable. I well remember that tired old list of six 'titles' chalked on the blackboard each term by my own art teacher, and there are art rooms today where the only generator for the work is a predictable and dusty still-life group or a pile of magazines.

Good talk, genuine dialogue between teacher and child, discussion and interaction between children, real investigation – all these are hallmarks of good teaching in whatever subject. In the teaching of art they are as essential as the variety of visual resource material you will find in most art rooms.

Resources – Range and Access

The collection, organization and use of resource material is an important part of your work as an art teacher. Every art teacher has to be a magpie – the kind of person who can't pass by a builder's skip without looking in to see what other people are throwing away!

Although art teachers adopt different styles in the presentation and use of their rooms – ranging from the happy cluttered junk shop to the well ordered visual laboratory – they all need to provide a battery of visual resource material of all kinds and some kind of system to ensure that children and staff are able to find and use it easily.

In Example 6, a teacher describes how she manages and organizes the room for which she is responsible – how she uses resources and presentation in different kinds of ways within the room as a support for the children's 'working and looking'.

I aim to provide an interesting and happy place for children to work in; a place which has a reasonable sense of order and where children are encouraged to be responsible and sensitive in their attitude to resources and equipment; a place where there are always interesting things to look at and talk about and where visual source material helps the children in their looking and thinking.

Note how the art room is used to create different kinds of space for the following: reference (thinking and planning), resource collections, special thematic displays, general display of children's work, clean and mucky working areas etc. All art teachers need to have their own collections of resources to support their own particular way of working. These will reflect

Fig. 3.8   Corridor with wheel chairs; mixed media
(56 × 75cm).

Fig. 3.9.   Children's ward; mixed media (60 × 82cm).

Fig. 3.10   Two wheel chairs; pencil and charcoal
(56 × 72cm).

*Work by 15-year-olds resulting from the opportunity to
work intensively for four days, when the first two days
were spent working and making studies in the Royal
Devon and Exeter Hospital, followed up by two days of
studio work at Exeter College of Art and Design.*

individual taste and idiosyncrasies. It is always pleasant to visit a large art department and to see a variety of visual environments within one unit. In bigger departments, it is necessary to have some kind of overall policy for the use and distribution of resource materials – both to avoid too much duplication from room to room and to ensure that reference material is easily and quickly available.

Whether you are working in a one-teacher department, co-ordinating the work of several teachers in a middle school, or running a large department in a secondary school, it is important to create a resources or reference area so that children can have easy and independent access to the variety of resource material they will need, especially when they begin to work more individually and with much more personal choice of content.

Primary Source Material

The importance of using direct experience as the basis for much of our work with children does make it essential to have as rich a collection of natural and man-made forms as your art room will accommodate. Example 6, and all those other examples which describe teaching projects, between them provide ample evidence of the range of resources that may be used to support your work with children.

Although natural and man-made forms will frequently be used independently, as useful and intriguing things in their own right and that are worthy of close study, they are most effectively used when they are grouped and organized and placed in conjunction with other reference material, to explain or to illustrate the possibilities within one particular idea or concept, for example:

colour range and relationships;
the ordering of pattern and its relationship;
metamorphosis from one form to another;
change and decay;
distortion;
light and reflections; etc.

Studies from man-made forms. Examples of children working from some of the rich variety of man-made forms that are available as source material.

Fig. 3.11   Jars filled with string; chalks and charcoal (82 × 56cm). 15-year-old, Burrington School, Plymouth.

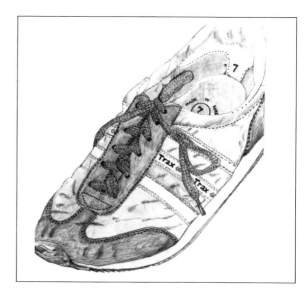

Fig. 3.12   Training shoes; coloured pencils (21 × 28cm). 13-year-old, Elize Hele School, Plympton.

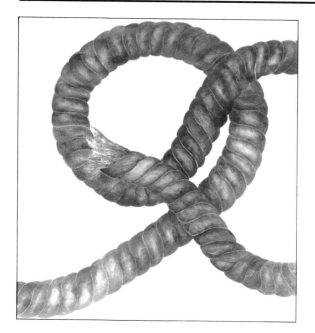

Fig. 3.13   Rope; pencil (40 × 53cm). 15-year-old, Audley Park School, Torquay.

Fig. 3.14   Kingfisher; water-colour and pencil (25 × 25cm). 17-year-old, Exeter College.

Examples of children working from a variety of natural forms, where they have been particularly motivated by the challenge of recording in detail those subtleties of surface and pattern that can be found in the variety of animal and plant forms that are available for their study.

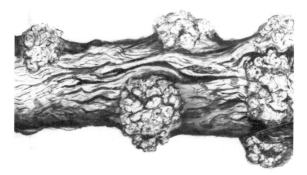

Fig. 3.15   Branch covered with lichen; water-colour and pencil (25 × 60cm). 13-year-old, Axminster School.

Fig. 3.16   Two cats; pencil (30 × 24cm). 14-year-old, Exmouth School.

79

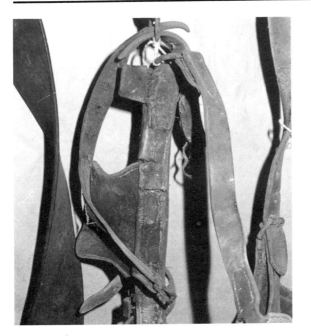

Fig. 3.17   Horse's bridle.

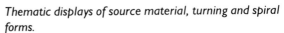

Thematic displays of source material, turning and spiral forms.

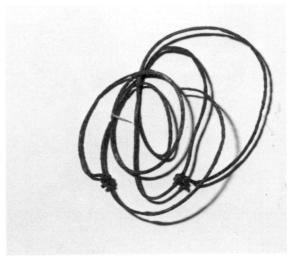

Fig. 3.19a   Wire Springs

Fig. 3.18   Lawn mower.

Fig. 3.19b   Seaweed

Thematic displays of source material, metamorphosis.

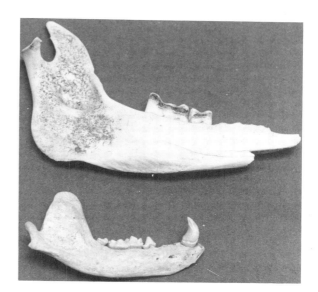

Fig. 3.20   Shoes and jaw bones.

Fig. 3.21   Bicycle saddle.

(Figures 3.11–3.22 show some of the uses of combinations of natural and man-made forms together with secondary source materials to illustrate different concepts.)

For example, a display intended to give children some understanding of the basic properties of one colour could contain any or all of the following:

selection of plants;
swatches of material in different shades of green;
colour charts made up from magazine sources;
painters' and decorators' colour charts;
group of everyday green objects;
fruits and vegetables;
samples of different coloured papers;
reproductions of several paintings that have a green bias;
branches and stones covered with lichen;
etc.

Everyday and familiar things may be used to generate more expressive work as well as the more usual objective work. Familiar things placed in unusual context – as, for example, when they appear out of scale, lit imaginatively, reflected or distorted in different kinds of surfaces or placed in an unusual juxtaposition – may all trigger off unusual or personal responses in children (figures 3.23–3.25).

The natural and man-made world come together most dynamically outside the school. Each school is contained within an environment or community that has its own particular or peculiar qualities, in which the activity of man manifests itself in different ways. Some environments are developed slowly over a long period of time, and the recording of that change can provide a valuable source for your work with children. Some, like the new shopping centre or housing estate, are virtually ready-made – but

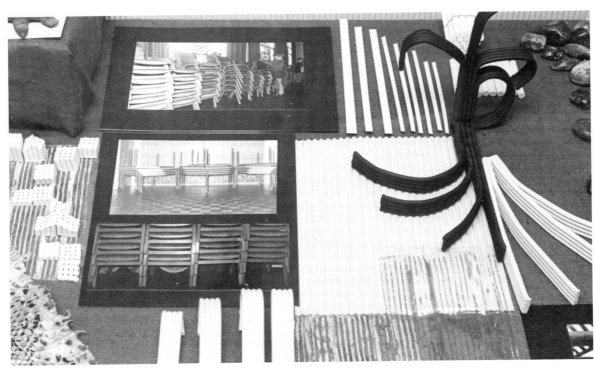

Fig. 3.22   Pattern display, general view.   *Thematic display of source material.*

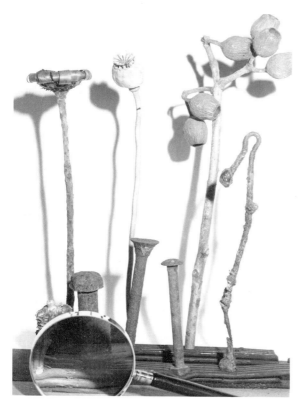

Displays of familiar things placed in unusual context in order to trigger off personal responses in children.

Fig. 3.23 (top left) Natural and man-made plants.

Fig. 3.24 (top right) Natural and man-made horns.

Fig. 3.25 Transistor and coral.

even the most boring housing estate can be studied to record the way it is used by the people who live in it. A housing estate can be visually coded to show:

what colours people paint it;
what eccentric or personal additions they add to their properties;
how they plan and use their gardens;
how different kinds of people move within it;
etc.

Much useful research into the use of the man-made environment came through the Schools Council/Arts Council project 'Art and the built environment' and its associated publications.

The school itself can be an exciting visual source: as a three-dimensional structure housing many activities and hundreds of people, at various kinds of work, it offers rich variety; it is divided into different sections for different kinds of activities; it is built of materials which support, divide, protect, move, decorate, cover and join; it contains forms which are coloured, patterned, solid, reflecting, soft, hard, regular, irregular etc.

The school houses children who are interesting source material in themselves. Children are all different from each other, they move differently, wear different things, make noises, pull faces, interact, change shape, squash into small spaces, expand into larger ones, play games, make things, order and disorder etc.

You and your colleagues are interesting source material to children because of the things you wear, your idiosyncrasies and your likes and dislikes. The children's response to the teachers who demonstrated to them evidence of their own past, in the teaching project, described in Example 3 of Chapter 2, 'Time past', is an example of the way that teachers might occasionally use themselves as subjects for visual study by their pupils.

There is so much first-hand source material available to use in art teaching, the main problem is not so much what to work from today, but how to ensure that over a period of time a reasonable balance is kept between the use of natural, man-made, environmental and personal resources.

Secondary Source Material

In addition to real things, places, people and events, there is a vast range of secondary source material available which illustrates or reproduces evidence of the world in which we live. By far the most important of these are works of art, craft and design – both existing forms and their reproduction in photograph or on film. Because of the importance of this group, they are dealt with separately in Chapter 6, 'Using works of art'. There is no doubt that children learn a great deal from the study and appraisal of the work of other artists, and that this can have significant influence upon the range and quality of their studio work.

The dominant secondary source material available to us is the photograph. The considerable growth of the communications industry, and its accompanying wealth of photographic source material, has been both a boon and a problem to art teachers over the past two decades. On the bonus side has been the valuable increase in the quantity and range of reference material available through photographic material in books, magazines and colour supplements. This has made it possible for the diligent teacher to give pupils, through collecting, sorting and cataloguing photographic sources, a very comprehensive visual reference library at comparatively little cost. Where the reference material is well organized for easy reference, this can provide children with access to valuable visual information, especially in support of work which is demanding or complex in content.

The technical improvements made in colour reproduction in magazine photography has also provided both teachers and children access to a rich range of colour source material, and there have been many examples of this kind of source material being well used in the study of colour in association with painting. These are discussed further in Chapter 5, 'Painting as an extension of drawing'.

Examples of children's use of the environment as source material for their work – ranging from the familiar environment of the home to environments farther afield.

Fig. 3.26 My garden; lino cut (20 × 15cm). 12-year-old, Park School, Barnstaple.

Fig. 3.27 Staircase at home; pencil (37 × 42cm). 17-year-old, Plymouth High School for Girls.

Fig. 3.28 Bison at Paignton Zoo; pencil (26 × 36cm). 15-year-old, Torquay Girls' Grammar School.

Fig. 3.29 Sheep on Dartmoor; tempera colour (56 × 76cm). 16-year-old, Ivybridge School.

Children using themselves as source material. Two contrasting portraits – one an introspective self portrait, the other a vigorous view of a friend.

Fig. 3.30   Self portrait; water-colour (28 × 38cm). 16-year-old, Clyst Vale College.

Fig. 3.31   Portrait of a friend; ink (41 × 60cm). 17-year-old, Okehampton School.

The problems associated with this growth of photographic source material lie more within the temptation it offers for teachers and children to seek an easy and superficial short cut towards making impressive images simply through the automatic copying of attractive source material. In recent years there has been a much needed return to primary source material in many schools, but there are still some art departments where easy and superficial access – especially to the colour supplements and pop magazines – does result in an excess of copying. It is a depressing sight to watch a class of 15-year-olds sifting half-heartedly through a stack of magazines in search of an image to copy!

The use of this kind of source material has been supported and justified in the light of two significant developments in the visual arts – the 'pop art' and 'photo-realism' movements.

Although the pop art movement had a viable philosophy and the result of focusing the work of artists more upon contemporary source material, its transfer into the schools has been at the rather superficial level of making fashionable the aping of images from 'popular' culture. There is a considerable difference between encouraging children to use their art to survey themselves and their own culture seriously, and simply allowing them to copy the slick images designed to sell the latest fashion or record to teenagers.

There is no doubt that photographic source material can be used constructively – to provide children with information about things they want to draw and paint for which it is almost impossible to provide them with real experience. Good photographs of such things as camels, racing cars and mountain ranges can usefully support the search for visual information.

A crucial factor here is the way in which access to photographic source material is determined by the drawing or painting problem that is presented to the children. It is a viable task to ask the children to find three photographs of very contrasting characters and to use these to create an image in which these contrasts are expressed (figure 3.32). It makes undoubted sense to encourage the children to make their own photographic records of things they particularly want to draw or paint or model. It may be intriguing to the children to ask them to compare the contrast between photographs of water, effects of water in reproductions of paintings and the way in which water is painted in original paintings. Many visual things we might require children to observe are so transitory – as in the movement of clouds, water or people – that photographs which 'freeze' the phenomenon can be a valuable support to their observation.

Occasionally there may be photographs which are so powerful in their meaning and quality that they do genuinely stir in children a desire to express a similar meaning in their own work. We have to acknowledge the fact that certain images act as ikons for children and may genuinely motivate them to pursue an equivalent meaning in their own image-making.

The way in which you use photographic source material can have a very significant bearing upon the nature of your work with children. The question that always has to be asked is to what extent access to this kind of source material is essential to the children's image-making. Will it help them in pursuit of their own response to the task you have set them? Will such reference enlarge their perception of the images they want to make?

Similarly, there are question marks about the use of the source material available through books and publications. It is obviously necessary for children to have access to a wide variety of publications that illustrate the work of other artists – great masters, contemporary artists, illustrators, graphic designers and craftsmen. Such source material can be invaluable where it is used to demonstrate the variety of solutions that artists have discovered to the representation of different kinds of content. Many children find inspiration within the work of particular artists whose vision enlarges their own understanding of things they have seen and wish to represent. It is important here to encourage children to be catholic in their use of source material and to challenge those who seem to be too content to use indiscriminately the work of one particular artist or designer. The greater the variety of artists' work you present to children – through photographs, publications and slides – the more likely they are to find ways of working that satisfy their own individual needs to represent the world as they see and feel it.

It is not insignificant that those art departments that most clearly develop a 'house style' – where the bulk of the children's work tends to conform to a particular kind of content or way of working – are those very departments where the only work displayed is that by the children themselves. It is all too easy for children to respond very quickly to the apparent expectations of an art teacher through observing that work which is publicly displayed for approval. The fewer alternatives they are faced with the more likely they are to assume that certain ways of working are acceptable. It is in these circumstances that 'school art' becomes the main determinant for children's image-making, at the expense of the enormous fund of source material that can be found in the work of artists, designers and craftsmen through the ages.

Other Art Forms

Children's work in the visual arts can be strengthened and supported through reference to and use of work in the other arts – literature, poetry, music and drama. The quality of observation that many writers and poets have brought to their perceptions of the world can frequently help children to key into the particular meaning and quality of things that they see and experience. There are many examples in this book, within the

Fig. 3.32 Three people at the bus stop; water-colour and pencil (30 × 43cm). 15-year-old, Dawlish School. *This is a good example of the constructive use of photographic source material. In this painting, the student has taken photographs of three contrasting characters as the starting point for a composition and has tried to place them in a setting and relationship where those contrasts are expressed.*

Fig. 3.33 Okehampton railway bridge; tempera colour (40 × 64cm). 16-year-old, Okehampton School. *Photographs can be valuable source material, especially when working from the local environment. This painting is based upon photographs taken by the student himself and shows how using photography, as the initial exploration to a painting, can help the student focus upon and 'frame' part of the environment he finds particularly rewarding.*

Children working directly from photographs. Although copying of this kind is useful mainly as a technical exercise in drawing, it can have additional value where the image chosen has real meaning and significance for the child who uses it.

Fig. 3.34   Cat; pencil (22 × 26cm). 15-year-old, Audley Park School, Torquay.

Fig. 3.35   Downs syndrome child; pencil (31 × 45cm). 16-year-old, Okehampton School.

descriptions of teaching projects, where art teachers have made good use of literature, poetry and music in support of their work. The use of this kind of source material, and the working links that might be established between the arts, are discussed in more detail in Chapter 8, 'Art and other subjects'.

Display and Presentation of Children's Work and Source Material

It has to be taken for granted that art departments play a major part in creating some kind of visual ethos in the schools they serve. It is normally expected that the bulk of children's work displayed in public areas of the school will come from the art department. It is important to try to make more of this routine demonstration of the work of the department than standard window dressing. Obviously the children's work should be well displayed — well mounted, occasionally framed and presented — to make the most capital from this opportunity to demonstrate the work of the department.

A good public display of children's work can help to explain to your colleagues and to the children themselves that quality of looking and thinking that supports the production of the end-products. The display of children's work makes much more sense where the finished work is placed alongside the various kinds of source material that generated the work. When this is accompanied by some outline notes which explain the thinking and direction behind the work, together with examples of those preliminary studies and investigations which supported the enquiry, you are much more likely to convince your colleagues that the production of images and artefacts is the result of serious and intelligent investigation. The more you can use the advantages of being continually required to demonstrate publicly the work of your department, the more likely you are to be able to make a cast iron case for the place and importance of your subject within the school curriculum.

EXAMPLE 1

EXAMPLE 1

'Tones and tunnels' – a first-year project

John Broomhead   *Head of Art Department, Great Torrington School*

This project outline is usefully divided into three sections: teacher activity, pupil activity and resources/materials. Note the use of different teaching ploys and methods and the accompanying questionnaire which encourages surmise and speculation. (See pages 70–71.)

First-year project: Tones and tunnels

Answer the questions below in your sketchbooks.
Use the heading 'Living caves' and do not forget the date!

1　What different types of tunnels and caves are there?
2　What are these caves and tunnels made in?
3　Make lists of both man-made and natural tunnels – what would be the main difference between the two?
4　What tunnels have you been in – describe your experience.
5　How would you *feel* about spending a long time living in a tunnel?
6　What would you do to exist – eat, keep warm etc?
7　Would the inside of a tunnel smell?
8　What noises might you hear?
9　What would the sides of a tunnel feel like if you touched them?
10　Would *you* feel hot or cold?
11　What creatures may live in tunnels – real or imaginary?
12　How do they move around?
13　Do they live in the roof, floor, crevices, entrance to the tunnel, or, deep down in its depths?
14　How do these creatures find their way around dark caves and tunnels?

Teacher activity	Pupil activity	Resources and materials
Section I: Tone		
Introduce Tone. Take examples of children's property (pencil case, bags, socks, books etc.) plus items from art studio. Compare and distinguish to aid understanding of differences between Tone and Colour. Touch upon 'differences' within one colour, e.g. lemon yellow, brill. yellow, orange/yellow, creamy yellow, grey/yellow.	Sub-groups of 4: to collect objects of same colour, but different tones. Attempt to arrange in order from light to dark.	Black and white/coloured photographs. Range of coloured objects around the room. Colour charts.
Compare black and white photographs with colour. Focus attention upon subtlety of tones to achieve detail and form in black and white examples.	Class discussion: children study photographs and identify areas where a wide range of tones are employed.	Good selection of photographs.
Present range of pencils. Discuss, question, 6B–6H grades, graphite/clay content, different purpose etc. Instructions to make simple tonal grid (12 squares).	Class discussion and experiment: children compare the *feel* and result of using different grades of pencil.	Sets of pencils.
	Individual: to make tonal grid ranging from white to black in 12 steps, using 6 different grades of pencil.	Squared paper.

EXAMPLE I

Section II: Caves and Tunnels

Using tables, chairs, boxes, make simple tunnels – wide, narrow, low, high, straight, windy. Briefly present and discuss knowledge re caves and tunnels. Is there a difference between the two? Discuss feelings, posture, claustrophobia. How do we move? Does the limited space influence how we move and the speed at which we move?	Tables, chairs, tea chests.
Class activity: role play, how might we move through different types of tunnels. Class discussion re feelings, posture, speed of movement etc. Discuss feelings evoked by Henry Moore's drawings/painting of miners and underground scenes during the War.	Photographs of tunnels and caves. Henry Moore's drawings/paintings.
Alert pupils to where we may find tunnels, differences in scale, varied purpose and methods of construction. Look and ask for children's own experiences in caves and tunnels, encourage talking to whole group.	
Sub-groups: briefly list answers to questions opposite. Individual: move into questionnaires – class discussion as introduction – followed by written answers for homework.	Questionnaires/sketchbooks.

Section III: Looking and Drawing

Make available a wide range of objects, natural and man-made; shells, fungi, machine parts etc. Demonstrate how these can be arranged using plasticine, house bricks, viewfinders, mag. lens to create varied viewpoints.	Objects for drawing, mag. lens, house bricks, viewfinders, Plasticine.
Working in pairs: to select and arrange objects, and find small tunnels and caves running through, suitable for observed drawing. Drawings to be made individually using pencil. No shading. Emphasize in the drawings the 'entrances' to the tunnels.	Sketchbooks, range of pencils.
Emphasize selection and looking before drawing begins.	Objects for reference.
Individual work: using observed drawings from previous week, make a drawing of (i) a tall thin tunnel (ii) a wide, low tunnel (iii) a long curving tunnel. Use Tone to describe depth and interior of tunnels. Find simple ways to indicate scale by adding backgrounds of buildings, mountains, insects, creatures etc.	Photographs of caves, landscapes etc.

Section IV: Cave Animals

Present and ask for examples of animals living in caves. Identify a few. Why do these animals live in caves? Have they adapted to cope with this type of environment? If so, how have they adapted? Compare and discuss drawings.	Class discussion/question and answer.	Books, photographs.
Make drawings of cave dwelling creatures.		Paper, pencil, coloured crayon.
Explain and demonstrate how real creatures can be changed into more exotic and mysterious creatures but still 'suitable' for cave living. Touch upon angry, friendly etc. Do not push too far with *all* children. RESPECT THEIR LEVEL OF UNDERSTANDING AND OWN IDEAS.	Invent unusual creatures but *always* working from the real towards the new. Write a few words about the new creature. Even give it a name.	Examples of illustrations from children's books showing strange creatures.

Section V: Relief Constructions

Demonstrate meaning of 'relief work', how it can be achieved using card. Emphasize and place value upon 'making' skills, the importance of good craftsmanship. Relate to local potters, Dartington glass etc.	Individual work but acting as a pair for mutual support: take previous drawings of caves and develop by using relief techniques as described opposite.	Glue. Corrugated card. Emulsion paint.
How to use real objects (shells, bark, logs, lichen, cork etc.) as a basis for designing textures for cave walls. Remind pupils how to describe scale by including a 'known' subject.	Paint emphasizing tone and texture – to provide feeling of depth. Varied brush techniques, wax crayons and pencil crayons. Develop previous ideas of cave creatures and make an idea using card and paint. These to be positioned within cave structure to indicate the scale/size of the cave, e.g. insect size, giant size.	Powder paint/PVA medium. Wax crayons, pencil crayons. 'Cave resources', natural objects, 'animal resources'.
Outline the whole project and place value upon individual achievements.	Explain, discuss work. Display, record. Assess.	Recording and assessment sheets.

EXAMPLE 2

EXAMPLE 2

A project on light

Robert Clement
Keith Hicks   *Headmaster, Ottery St Mary Primary School*
Peter Reid   *Whipton Barton Middle School, Exeter*
Jackie Ross   *Head of Expressive Arts Department, Queen Elizabeth
                School, Crediton*
Alma Yea   *Seaton Primary School*

This project was designed as part of the 'Sight Seekers'
programme in which teachers from primary, middle and
secondary schools worked together on the preparation of
curriculum material for use with children in the 9–12 age range.
The programme was directed by Neil White, ex-Art Advisory
Teacher for Devon and now Art Adviser to the London Borough
of Hillingdon (see pages 70–71).

The work is generally sequential but sequence should not
be pursued doggedly.

Many of the activities lead naturally into making art, others
are to do more with looking, seeing and investigating
materials. Some activities are complete in themselves and
may not lead themselves to further expression.

Many of the resources are scrap. There must be a lot of
resources – visual and material – but not so much that the
child is baffled and flits from one piece of material to
another. The children can supply lots of it – sweet papers,
silver foil etc. – and should be encouraged to collect and
discover their own.

Take trouble in collecting and setting out the stimuli and
resources. Watch that the children don't just 'lick the icing
off the cake'.

Preparation   It is important to make some preparation for this project. All
the various materials and visual resource material that you
will need should be easily and readily available.

Looking and focusing aids
Slide projector or overhead projector
Coloured Cellophanes and gelatines

Torches
Candles
Mirrors
Reflecting surfaces – spoons; jam jars; shiny paper etc.
Different kinds of glasses – polaroid; coloured; coloured
    bottles; frosted; reeded
Kaleidoscope
Lenses of various kinds
Magnifying glasses
Viewfinders

Materials
White paper – cartridge; newsprint; tracing paper; tissue
Black paper
Grey paper
Magazines
Paint
Charcoal
Crayons
Pastels
Chalk
Black ink
Heelball
Shiny and reflecting materials – foil; cigarette papers; sweet
    papers; Cellophane; plastic bags; plastic sheet etc.
Scissors
Knives
Cottons
String
Cardboard
Old boxes
Various containers – yoghurt pots; cartons; tins etc.
Tubes and cylinders
Strawboard
Junk materials for constructions

Visual resources
You will need to collect and display visual resources for the
children to look at and which will serve as the focus for their
looking and talking. These should include:
Photographs – different kinds of natural light; sunrise; sunset;
    dusk; brilliant sunlight; mist etc.; directional light; strong
    dark and light contrasts
Objects with light reflecting, distorting and shiny surfaces.
Fabrics and papers with a variety of surfaces.

EXAMPLE 2

Papers, fabrics, tissues, plastics, through which light will
pass.
(These should, if possible, be arranged against windows to
show how different materials diffuse and change light.)
These visual resources and objects should be simply
grouped and displayed in the classroom to generate specific
kinds of looking and discussion. Some simple things are
often enough more effective than over elaborate and fussy
displays, e.g.
Paperclips scattered on shiny paper
A pile of tins against a mirror
Xmas baubles on black plastic
Leaf skeletons against a window etc.

Initial activities   **Focusing attention upon different aspects of light**

LOOKING   TALKING   INTERACTION

The following activities might take up one or two afternoons.
You can do any of them in any order. How many you attempt
will depend upon the response from your class and what
other kinds of talk and looking the activities encourage
children to determine for themselves. Some of these
activities depend upon certain light or weather conditions. It
is best if the children work in small groups – two or three at a
time working on different activities.

   (i) Choose an object. Look at it in a box, on the windowsill,
out of doors. Describe how its appearance changes
under these different conditions.

  (ii) Hold up a large leaf against the sky – hold it against the
ground.
What do you notice about the colour?

 (iii) Where does the sky stop looking blue?

 (iv) Make a little frame viewfinder. Look through it and
'capture' the lightest picture you can find and the
darkest picture you can find in the school playground.
Notice where they are.
Make a map or diagram to show the lightest and
darkest parts of the playground.

  (v) Find a place where you can see a long way. Describe
the colour of the building nearest to you and the colour
of those farthest away. Compare the colour of the trees
nearest to you with those farthest away.

(vi) Can you half close your eyes and make things look blurred? What do you notice? Which colours appear to stand out most?

(vii) Look at windows of the school and of houses nearby. Look at the windscreens of cars parked nearby. What are they reflecting today?

(viii) Look at your face – in a shiny spoon, in a goldfish bowl, reflected in a window. How does it change? Is it lighter, darker, different colours?

(ix) (On a sunny day) Stand on one spot in the playground and get your friend to draw round your shadow with a piece of chalk. Go back to the same spot an hour later and see if your shadow has changed. Repeat at intervals during the day.

(x) Look at the way faces change when they are lit by a torch – from the left-hand side, from the right-hand side, from below, from above.

(xi) Look at the view through the window, through a plastic bag, through a piece of muslin, through your half open fingers, through a cardboard cylinder. Describe how it is different each time.

(xii) Place two or three familiar objects on a piece of white paper. By shining a torch on the objects from different directions, see how much you can change the shape of the shadows.

Collecting, finding and using resources

The following three activities are included to involve the children in selecting and collecting resources they might use. Each could be attempted by a small group of children – to run parallel with the looking and talking activities above. It may be necessary to plan for this to take place over a period of time to allow time for children to find and collect things. The whole class can be involved in the finding and collecting.

(i) These are all words which can be used to describe different kinds of light:

murky translucent frosted hazy shimmering dazzling smoky silhouetted glowing glaring sparkling dappled deflected gloomy flickering.

Make a collection of pictures, or sections from pictures (using viewfinders), to illustrate these different kinds of

EXAMPLE 2

light. Make a nice arrangement of the words and pictures together.

(ii) Make a corner into a light and colour corner by placing different kinds of materials against the windows and on a table below the window and a variety of objects on the table. Choose a window which gets plenty of sun so that at different times of the day your corner will change light and colour as the sunlight changes.

(iii) Different kinds of surfaces reflect or absorb light. Make a collection of papers, materials, natural and man-made objects which are all a similar colour (red, blue or green are probably the easiest). Arrange them in an interesting way.

Recording light in tone and colour

Making light and dark
Divide the class into five groups. Give each group (or table) one of the following:

(i) Magazines and newspapers.
(ii) White chalk and charcoal; black, white and grey paper.
(iii) White and black crayons; black, white and grey paper.
(iv) White and black powder paint; black, white and grey paper.
(v) Black ink; white and grey paper.

Ask each group, collectively, to make as many different tones (or shades) between black and white using the materials they have on their table as they can.
Group with magazines and newspapers to find and cut out as many tones as they can.

A preliminary instruction is necessary to demonstrate how to make different tones mixing ink and water in different proportions, and to show that tones look different depending whether they are made on white, grey or black paper.

Allow 30–45 minutes for 'tone making'. Groups then to be asked to arrange all the tones they have made or found in tonal sequence from light to dark.

Detailed discussion about the different qualities of tones made with different media. Get children to identify different tones in the displays and resources in the classroom.

Shiny surface
Each child to have a shiny or reflecting surface or object:

Spoon
Tin can

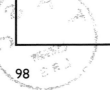

Mirror
Scrap of foil
Bottle
etc.

Children to move and turn and adjust their object until they see reflected in it interesting patterns of light and dark shapes.

Children to record the pattern of light and dark using chalk, charcoal, crayons, black and white paint working on grey paper.

Some emphasis upon the way the pattern of light and dark fits onto their reflecting shape – their drawing may be spoon-shaped, or mirror-shaped, or bottle-shaped etc.

Self portrait in a shiny surface?

Dark and light places

Children – using viewfinders – to explore the school grounds to find their favourite 'light picture' or 'dark picture'.

Make drawings – light pictures, pencil/charcoal on white paper.

– dark pictures, chalk/charcoal on grey paper.

Those children who have chosen the same view or area to work together on a collage of their light/dark picture using newspapers, magazines, fabric scraps etc. to define main areas of the picture, then to paint and draw over as needed.

Light and dark shapes

Set up against windows or against light, groups and collections of interesting objects with subtle differences:

Row of apples
Several bottles with different shapes
Branches
Shoes
etc.

Detailed talk about the differences between the shapes – where they are fattest, thinnest, straightest, most curved, solid, fragile etc.

Children to cut and tear shapes of one group of objects in black paper placed against white or in white paper placed against black.

To look at shapes again with detailed discussion about subtleties within the silhouette – where it is darkest, lightest, most patterned, roughest, smoothest etc.

EXAMPLE 2

Children to draw or paint over their silhouettes to complete their pictures.

Imaginative paintings
'Me in the dark'
'My house by moonlight'
'Dazzled by snow'
'A creature seen dimly' etc.

Looking at light changing and reflecting

Colour changing
Ask children to choose one of the primary colours and then, by adding white or black, to see how many variations they can make of that colour. (It will be easier for them to work from white/colour/black.)

Insist that they make at least *ten* different shades.

Over a period of time, children to note and record colour changes taking place around them:

Sky
Water
Leaves
Reflections (in puddles and windows)
Things left in strong light etc.

Colour/light diffusing
Children to observe changes in colour caused by changes in lighting and circumstances and to make appropriate studies in paintings/collage:

Pebbles in water
Houses in the rain
Fields at morning and evening
Faces by torchlight
Objects by candlelight
Familiar views through coloured spectacles etc.

Light and colour
(i) Experiments to explain how colour may be made by placing dabs and splodges of different colours close together:

make rubbings of different surfaces using
– red crayon on yellow paper
– white crayon on green paper
– yellow crayon on blue paper etc.

Observe these from different distances to see what is the overall colour effect.

(ii) Experiment with colour dabbing using sponges or big brushes to make 'patch' colour patterns
– two colours together
– three colours together
– four colours together.

(iii) Observation of broken colour effects in:

Birds' feathers
Pebbles
Birds' eggs
Moths
Fungi
Fruits
etc.

(iv) Recording from direct observation colour patterns or tonal patterns in any of the above using as appropriate small brushes and paint, felt pens, crayons on white paper, charcoal and chalks on grey paper etc.
Children to be asked to make studies larger in scale than the objects they are observing.

(v) Observation and discussion about paintings and photographs where effects of light and atmosphere are obtained by using broken colour effects, as in paintings by Seurat, Van Gogh, Constable, Turner, Pissaro, Bonnard, Manet etc.

(vi) Children to have some direct experience of effects of broken light and colour by walking through or under trees in strong sunlight, observing light glittering on water, looking at gardens full of flowers, watching rain or snow falling, staring into fires etc.

(vii) Children to make paintings using broken patterns of colour and light on themes appropriate to time of year:

Autumn leaves falling
Bonfires burning
Mists swirling
Snow falling
Rain storms
Clouds scudding
Spring blossoming
Sun beating etc.

EXAMPLE 3

EXAMPLE 3

Two instructional workcards – how to make a kaleidoscope and infinity box

Designed for use in association with the 'Reflections pack', Devon Schools Museums Service (see page 71).

MAKE YOUR OWN- KALEIDOSCOPE

YOU WILL NEED - 2 plane mirrors and a piece of stiff black card all of the same size and sticky tape.

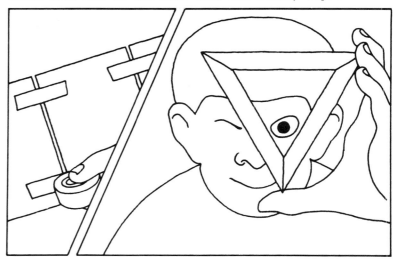

INSTRUCTIONS - tape the card and mirrors (facing inwards) together to form a tube and look through it.

DEVON SCHOOLS MUSEUM
SERVICE
33a Meadfoot Lane, Torquay
Telephone 25779

MAKE YOUR OWN- INFINITY BOX

YOU WILL NEED - 4 plane mirrors of the same size, sticky tape, fluorescent paper and a plastic figure (or other small object).

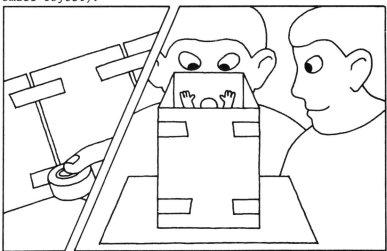

INSTRUCTIONS - tape the mirrors(facing inwards) together, stand them on the fluorescent paper and put the figure inside - look into the top of the box and see how many figures you can count.

DEVON SCHOOLS MUSEUM
SERVICE
33a Meadfoot Lane, Torquay
Telephone 25779

EXAMPLE 4

EXAMPLE 4

'Big and little' project sheets

This project was designed as part of the 'Sight Seekers' programme in which teachers from primary, middle and secondary schools worked together on the preparation of curriculum material for use with children in the 9–12 age range. The programme was directed by Neil White, ex-Art Advisory Teacher for Devon and now Art Adviser to the London Borough of Hillingdon. Note how the children's concept of 'Big and little' is supported by visual enquiry, talking and writing, and interaction (see pages 69–72).

talking and writing

REFERENCES

SLIDES

16. WATER TUNNEL

17. BIG ARCH

18. LADYBIRD

19. PEBBLE CAVE

also
13. Crater
14. Worm holes

DISPLAY TITLES

BIG & LITTLE
NEW VIEWS

OTHER

Mrs Pepperpot,

Gulliver,

Jack and the
Beanstalk

STARTERS

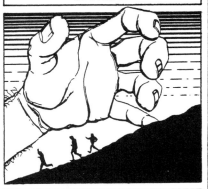

Be an insect describing a journey from your own chin to the top of your head, or through a hedge, or across a table etc.

Be a giant and describe how he sees you and your surroundings as you go home from school.

Consider the way you feel in different size spaces. Does looking at the stars make you feel small? Where do you feel big, small, confident nervous? What is it about the space around you that makes these different feelings?

Describe spaces that are happy/ frightening/comfortable/miserable but describe the space rather than the objects in the space.

POSSIBLE CONNECTIONS

INSECT BEHAVIOUR
MAPS
LENSES
THE UNIVERSE!
ILLUSIONS

explorations

SPACE WALK

Find and observe insects going about their normal business. Try and put yourself in their six shoes (or eight if a spider!)

Use magnifying glasses to get very close to where the insects live.

PEOPLE

Try out the feeling of being in very enclosed places – under tables, in boxes, in cupboards – compared with big places – out of doors, the school hall, a church. Describe in words or painting the different feelings, choosing two or three to concentrate on.

THINGS

Study maps and draw your own maps of particular places you know well – map incidents as well as appearances.

IDEAS CARDS

for classes,
for groups or
for individuals

1
Make a picture of a giant's eye view of a place you know well.

2
Draw a map of a dog for a flea
or
a map of part of your garden for a mouse
or
a map of your hand for a money spider,
or
. . . .

3
Choose a photograph to cut from a magazine. Now add some other cutouts to it to make the sizes "go wrong".

4
Make a person 15 cm high. Now build him or her a special place to live in which he or she will like.
Write about it too if you like.

EXAMPLE 5

EXAMPLE 5

Objective drawing worksheet

John Broomhead   *Head of Art Department, Great Torrington School*

A programme of objective drawing to be completed as homework in years 4 and 5 (see page 76).

OBJECTIVE DRAWING
WORK SHEET

The work set on this sheet is for you to complete at home, or in free study time.

You make make studies of either the whole or only part of the subject given.

Small specimens or details may be enlarged and aids such as magnifying lenses may be used.

Any media or mixed media may be used, except collage and montage.

The work is to be carried out in your sketch books.

GRADE

1. a) a dandelion or thistle or other spikey leafed plant with leaves and roots.
   b) a plant with large leaves.
   c) either several sticks of rhubarb with leaves, or several courgettes which may be cut open.

2. a) spectacles or sunglasses.
   b) two or more spanners, or similar tools.
   c) a bunch of keys.

3. a) bubbles on the surface of water.
   b) a lighted candle.
   c) a pile of ice cubes.

4. Very small objects enlarged, e.g. drawing pin, half-burnt matchstick, pencil sharpener, rubber band, ball bearing, safety pin, etc.

5. Looking through a key-hole, or slightly open door, or window with curtains half drawn.

6. At least four drawings describing your hand and/or your feet.

7. Slice in half a tomato/orange/cabbage or any other interesting
fruit or vegetable, and make a careful study.

8. a) a bicycle or pram.

   b) a car.

   c) the kitchen sink and surrounding area.

9. a) a pair of walking or climbing boots or old sandals,
      lying or standing on the floor.

   b) a untidy pile of old newspapers and magazines.

   c) a wind instrument with keys such as a saxaphone,
      clarinet or modern flute.

10. a) a pile of broken egg shells.

   b) an old skull.

   c) one or more fir cones.

11. Either make a detailed drawing of a twig with berries, or a
flower with leaves, paying particular attention to the joints
of stems and leaves.

12. A bottle, a shiny metal teapot, kettle, etc. Any reflective
surface. Try to capture the reflections.

13. A torch and battery.

14. Broad beans or peas with the pods open to show the inside,
or part of a bean or pea plant with pea pods forming.

15. Looking up a stairwell, or at buildings and trees, or a
view along a corridor, passage or path.

16. One or more spiked running shoes, hockey boots, or football boots.

17. A leafy branch of oak, ash, horse chestnut or other deciduous
tree.

18. A packet of biscuits or crisps partly opened showing some of
the contents falling out.

19. Handbag, sports bag or school bag, opened showing the contents
spilling out.

20. Orange, apple, banana, or similar fruit partly peeled and
opened showing the inside.

21. Close view of a large flower head, a cross section may be made.

22. Glass or clear bottle half filled with water.

23. 'Bottom of the garden'.

24. Random collection of objects from the kitchen, i.e. open tin
cans, dish cloth, dishes, tin opener etc.

25. Three different views of a cup and saucer.

26. Opened egg box.

27. Enlarged study or studies of a piece of jewellery, e.g. earings,
ring, etc.

EXAMPLE 6

EXAMPLE 6

My art room

Jean Coombe   *Head of Expressive Arts Department, Dawlish School*

In this extract, Jean is writing about the management of her room in her previous appointment at Paignton Lower School. A longer version of this extract was previously published in 'Art 7/11' (1978), an occasional paper from the Schools Council Art Committee (see page 76.)

I aim to provide an interesting and happy place for children to work in; a place which has a reasonable sense of order and where children are encouraged to be responsible and sensitive in their attitude to resources and equipment; a place where there are always interesting things to look at and talk about and where visual source material helps the children in their looking and thinking.

There is plenty of space in the art room – lots of working surfaces and interesting corners and display areas. I encourage the children to be mobile – to use all the space, to be curious about what is new in the room this week. There is movement of furniture to make different kinds of working spaces as the need arises, small scale or large scale depending upon the current projects.

Nearly all the equipment and materials is kept along one entire wall of the art room. Materials are arranged in such a way as to encourage sensible use. There are clearly defined areas for colour dispensing, cleaning palettes and brushes, glueing and sticking, printing, paper storage etc. I try to make things interesting – by storing powder paint in large glass jars so it is nice to look at, for example.

There is a working wall where children can put together collections of pictures, photographs, their own drawings, resources they have collected etc.; where they can work large scale if they want to or where several children can work together on a joint project.

There is a quiet and sectioned off thinking, planning, looking, researching work place. It contains a carpet, armchair, a low table, books, projection box, filing cabinet, magazine collection etc.; somewhere for the children to go to collect ideas, sort things out, or just quietly look at things which might spark off ideas and thoughts.

There is one special corner for all the different objects used as resource material. These are housed on open shelving units for easy access to encourage the children to handle and explore and to be curious about all the things there on a casual basis, as well as when objects are grouped and arranged for special projects. The unit contains all kinds of natural and man-made things, many of them collected by the children, and will always include:

plants, shells, bones, pebbles, driftwood, feathers, intriguing oddments of junk, old shoes, hats, bits of machinery, interesting man-made objects, bottles, glass, old tools etc.

Magnifying glasses and lenses are kept nearby to encourage the children to look closely at some things. Sometimes a special item will take pride of place for a while . . . an old sewing machine, a costume, a large pot, a carving from the Museum Service etc.

There are special display corners where specific collections or experiments are set up, usually with spotlighting, and these are used to support current projects, e.g.

A collection of objects, materials and reproductions all in a particular range of colour.
Shiny and reflecting objects displayed against mirrors and foil papers.
A collection of fruits and of pots and objects with similar shapes.
A camouflage exhibition.
etc.

In addition to using display spaces to reinforce current work, they are also used to display children's work – often in association with some of the visual source material that served to support it. It is important to display children's work well to reinforce their achievements and to give them confidence in the validity of their own work by making something special of its appearance.

I like to display children's work so that it makes some kind of overall sense as a unit – so that children from other classes, and my colleagues, can have some notion of what has been attempted and achieved by a particular group of children. Sometimes it is necessary to provide supporting notes or information to make it clear to the casual onlooker

EXAMPLE 6

what has been attempted or achieved by a group of children. The sequence of the display and its relationship to source material can often determine how well the work is understood and appreciated by others.

Other spaces in the school are useful resources for my own work. I make quite a lot of use of the School Hall – especially with children of lower ability – to give them direct experiences through drama which will reinforce the visual enquiries they are making in art. The library is easily available and I encourage children to use it for all kinds of simple research in association with their work in art.

The school building and grounds, the adjacent fields, the local church, the town centre – all these are used constantly as visual source material. Sometimes I will arrange children's drawings and paintings of the school and town environment together with reproductions of appropriate paintings by famous artists, so that the children will begin to see the relationship between their own drawing of a field or hedge and the work of Constable and Van Gogh. We have the enormous bonus of being within walking distance of a good zoo, and this also is used constantly as source material for children's work, as it is so rich in the range and variety of its forms.

Within my teaching I make a great deal of use of visual source material of all kinds. Much of this is because the bulk of my work is with first- and second-year children where there is a special need to give them as much real and direct experience as possible of the world about them, so as to begin to teach them how to look with discrimination and imagination.

4 TEACHING DRAWING

Everyone Can Draw

Children rarely say 'I can't draw' much before the age of eight. But when children do recognize that the drawings and images they make have public consequence, they begin to compare and relate their drawings to the appearance of the real world and all those other images of the real world that surround them in pictures and photographs and in film and television.

It is at this point that children need help and support from the teacher to make the 'real' images that will satisfy them. In very positive ways, you can provide the source materials, resources and help in looking and focusing that will encourage them to begin to describe and communicate through their drawings as well as to use them as a means of personal expression.

When children draw they are responding to different kinds of experience. What they draw and how well they draw will depend in a large measure upon the questions or problems you pose them. For example, the children's response to the problem of making an image of a house is determined by the way in which you present the task to them, by what questions you ask, by what experience you give them of the idea of a house.

If you ask the children to draw a house – any house – without any supporting talk or discussion, they will usually produce very standard stereotypes for a house – a rectangle, with a central door and a window in each corner and a triangle for its roof. Those with more mechanical dexterity will perhaps draw a more 'skilful' stereotype and may be confident enough to add a little more detail like a door knocker, or curtains or a garden path and fence. Even at thirteen or fourteen years of age, children will cheerfully resort to making 'six-year-old' stereotypes for houses when, as here, the task of drawing the house has not been properly defined or focused.

Talk to the same group of children about the houses they live in and, through discussion and questioning, draw from them verbal descriptions of differences between their houses, and then ask them to draw their *own* house, and their drawings will have more purpose and authenticity because the drawings are based upon some kind of experience – their ability to recall what their houses look like has been focused through talk and discussion.

Take the same group of children to a nearby terrace of houses and get them looking and talking, making notes, writing down words, making diagrams – beginning to identify how the houses are subtly different from each other – and it is even more likely that their drawings will have some authenticity.

Show the children a doll's house with the front removed so that they can see it in section, talk about this kind of view and then ask them to make a sectional drawing or diagram of their own house to show how it is lived in, and the quality and appearance of the drawing will change again.

Ask the children to invent the house that will house strange or mythical or funny creatures – especially those described in poetry or prose – and the drawings that follow will have a different kind of quality and purpose.

Give the children clip boards, graph paper, rulers and sharp pencils, sit them down before a row of houses and teach them to construct the façade of the house by using the front door as a module of measurement, and their drawings will again have a different purpose and quality.

These different ways of responding to and

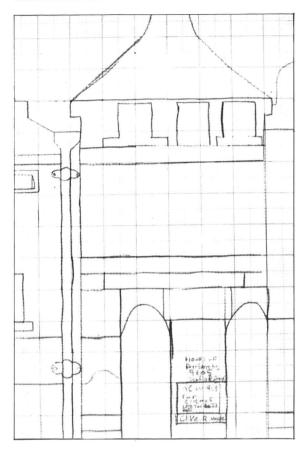

Fig. 4.1   Shop facade on Bideford Quay; pencil on graph paper (17 × 28cm). 10-year-old, Westcroft Junior School, Bideford. *Using graph paper as an aid to measurement when making drawings in which the accurate measurement of proportion and shape are necessary.*

recording the appearance of a house all have different and valuable functions. They involve the children in recording, analysis, conjecturing, imagining and communicating both ideas and information. It is essential that teachers understand and make positive use of the variety of ways of drawing that may be used to help children to be competent in their use of drawing, both to observe and to comment upon the world as they see it. The ability to draw is an essential tool of communication that can be taught to the vast majority of children. Drawing is not just a mystical gift of the favoured few – it is a useful educational tool that all children can learn to use.

Drawing is much more than acquiring the skills of accurate representation. It is not so much a skill to be learnt as a process to use for learning. Too often in schools the aim of drawing is to learn how to make drawings of those familiar and traditional objects that can be found in most art departments: wine bottles, Coca-Cola cans, bones and boots. It is not enough simply to teach children to draw drawings. One of the best ever descriptions of drawing came from an eight-year-old child who, when asked how he made a drawing, replied, 'I think and then I draw a line round my think.' This chapter draws together a wide range of tried and tested methods for helping children to think visually – and then to draw.

Drawing as Recording

The most objective function of drawing is where drawing is used to record – or describe – the appearance of things, either for the pleasure of knowing and recording them well or as the means for collecting information about the real world. The simple act of looking closely and carefully at real things provides a genuine stimulus for children and has much greater value than any amount of copying from existing pictures or from photographs.

When children are being asked to use drawing as a means to record the appearance and qualities of things seen in the environment, the teacher needs to provide support in two essential ways:

in the use of supporting talk and discussion;
by making available to the group those materials which best enable them to cope with the problem of recording.

Choice of Materials

Before starting any drawing with children, it is

important to give very careful thought to what materials should be used that will best help them to make an analogy in drawing media for the things they are observing, for example:

sharp hard pencils to draw small twigs and plants;
fine brushes and inks to draw black feathers;
chalk, charcoal and grey paper to draw a stone church;
coloured felt pens to draw a stained glass window etc.

Listed below are the most familiar drawing materials matched against those visual elements most easily recorded with them in order of effectiveness:

pencils (hard)	line	tone	texture	
pencils (soft)	tone	texture	line	
felt pen	line	colour		
Indian ink	line	texture	tone (when used with water)	
coloured inks	colour	tone	line	texture
wax crayon	colour	texture	line	
conte crayon	line	tone	texture	
charcoal	tone	texture	line	
water colour	colour	tone	line	
powder colour	colour	tone	texture	

Similar care should be given to the choice of paper, both for its colour and its size. Some subject matter will demand drawing on a very small scale using very sharp pencils or fine brushes, and others will demand a larger ground and the use of ink or paint with large brushes.

Helping children to explore the qualities and characteristics of different media is an important support to drawing. Experiments and exercises with different media can be very dull for pupils if taken out of context. Always use exploration for a specific task in drawing, so that the skills and

Four drawings showing good choice of media to observe close detail. These children have clearly been encouraged to explore the growth patterns of feather and hair with great care.

Fig. 4.2   Feather; white chalk on black ground (32 × 55cm). 12-year-old, Teignmouth High School.

Fig. 4.3   Back of the head; pencil (29 × 42 cm).
11-year-old, Exwick Middle School, Exeter.

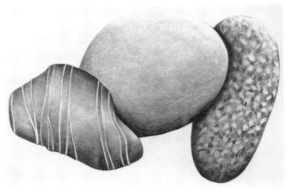

Fig. 4.5   Pebbles; pencil (35 × 25cm). 15-year-old,
Dawlish School.

Fig. 4.4   Old boots; pencil (42 × 48cm). 13-year-
old, Axminster School.

*These drawings showing particularly sensitive handling
of pencil in different ways. Note the vigorous use of
shading in the boots and the very subtle use of different
grades of pencil in the drawing of pebbles.*

qualities absorbed can be quickly and directly
used. For example, children should be asked to
experiment with HB, 2B and 3B pencils to discover their possible range of tone, before going
on to make careful studies of small pebbles and
shells, or to experiment with charcoal, black ink,
white paint and white chalk to see what textures
they will make in combination, before painting
and drawing domestic animals like rabbits or
pigeons.

Preliminary exercises to drawing a feather
should include the practice of making subtle
changes in tone with a variety of grades of pencil,
practising making gentle curves, practising placing curved lines very close to each other etc. This
kind of preparatory work will provide children
with more confidence in making the drawing.

Example 1 gives more detailed description of
the various ways that preliminary explorations
with materials can be directly linked to drawing.
If you concentrate on the use and choice of media
for specific drawing tasks, your pupils will see
that relationship between what they see and the
medium they are using.

Looking and Talking

The importance of talking – describing, questioning, discussing – as a support for drawing cannot
be overemphasized. It is through talk as much as

through looking that children come to see the world about them more clearly and perceptively. (Some of the ploys that can be used in association with looking have already been discussed in Chapter 3, 'Teaching strategies and resources'.)

Talk can be used in a variety of ways, the simplest being the way that a series of questions associated with looking can help children to see and select what is before them. For example, children looking at a feather which they are going to draw with pencils, and having made some experiments with different types of pencils, might be asked the following questions:

1 Where is the feather strongest?
2 Where is the quill thickest?
3 Where are the fibrils longest?
4 How wide is the base compared with the tip?
5 How is its length compared with its width?
6 How much does it curve?
7 Where does it curve most?
8 Where is it softest?
9 Where are the finest hairs?
10 Where is it dark?
11 Where is it light?
12 Where will you need to use a very fine point?
13 Where will you have to draw very delicately?
14 Where will you use your softest pencil?
15 Which part is most difficult to draw?
etc.

In this kind of description through questioning, look for differences and contrasts within the form that is being drawn so that children begin to see the subtleties that are there, always include questions about how the media might be used in this particular drawing (e.g. Questions 12, 13 and 14). Where the children have made preliminary experiments or exercises with the media, use these in association with the looking so that the children can identify directly techniques and effects that can be used to create the right analogy for the thing to be drawn.

An alternative to direct questioning is for you to make a detailed written questionnaire to help the children's looking, as in the 'Shoe question-naire' from Great Torrington School (Example 2) and the 'Myself questionnaire' from Paignton School (Example 3).

Encourage your pupils to observe more thoughtfully by asking them to talk to each other in pairs about what they see or to write down ten different words that describe the object they are to draw.

Comparisons

One of the simplest and most direct ways to help children to look is to place before them two similar things and to ask them to look for the differences between them – simple things like leaves or pebbles, complex things like two children who are similar in appearance. Comparison makes for careful observation, and children become conscious of subtleties of form, colour and surface. You can also help them to look by giving them an observation game to play, such as drawing one of their fingers so carefully that it is possible to identify straight away which finger has been drawn, or by sitting several children round a table to draw an eyebrow, nose or mouth of another so carefully that it can be quickly identified with its owner.

There are other more active forms of comparison. Using mirrors, children can observe how parts of their face change as they change expression. What happens to the eyebrow when it is raised or lowered in a frown? How does the mouth change as they pout, smile or snarl? They can be asked to make a series of drawings to show how a biscuit or an apple changes as they eat it, or what happens to a small lump of clay or Plasticine as it is pinched or pulled into different shapes.

A natural extension of this is to use drawing to explain how things change as they grow, develop and age. Ask pupils to bring to school photographs of themselves at different ages and to compare these with photographs and reproductions of paintings of people at different stages of life. Alternatively, they can make a series of drawings and studies over a period of time to

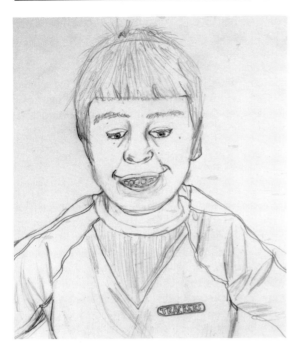

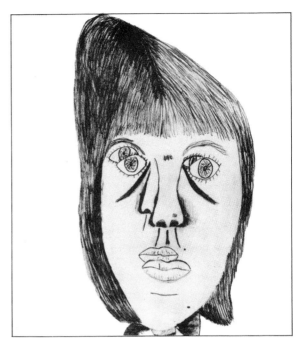

Figs 4.6 and 4.7   Portraits; pencil (24 × 42cm).
11-year-olds, Exwick Middle School, Exeter.

Figs 4.8 and 4.9   Self portraits through concave and
convex lenses; pencil. 12-year-olds, Vincent
Thompson High School, Exeter.

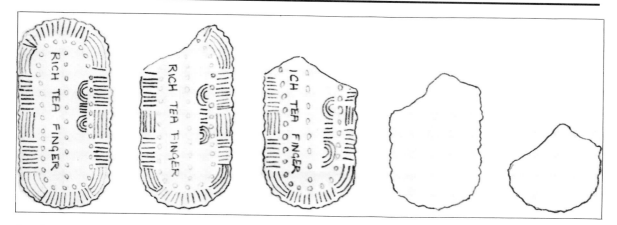

Fig. 4.10   Biscuit eating; pencil (9 × 25cm). 11-year-old, South Molton School.

Fig. 4.11   Felt pen distorted in glass of water; pencil (36 × 40cm). 17-year-old, Plymstock School.

Using changes in familiar things as a stimulus to careful observation.

describe the changes that take place in, for example, the growth of a bud to blossom, the transition from frog spawn to frog via tadpole, the changing forms of familiar fruits and vegetables as they rot and decay.

They can be asked to use drawings to examine polarities and to make comparisons between things that are:

rough and smooth;
old and new;
regular and irregular;
opaque and transparent etc.

Using comparisons between children in the class to encourage them to observe fine differences. The children compared themselves as seen in a mirror (Figs 4.6 and 4.7) and then in concave and convex lenses (Figs 4.8 and 4.9). Similar comparisons can be made using a shiny tablespoon.

Focusing

Where children are making studies from complicated forms — small studies of patterns and surfaces taken from a piece of driftwood, an eroded shell etc. — ask them to use a simple viewfinder — a small hole torn in a piece of paper — to select which bit they are going to draw and to isolate that part for special attention. Instead, they might use a rectangle cut in a piece of card like a camera viewfinder to select part of a landscape, a row of houses, a group of people, part of a room etc. that they are to draw. Here it is important that the shape of the drawing paper relates to the shape of the viewfinder so that what is seen through the viewfinder can be made to fit on to the piece of paper.

Children enjoy using irregularly shaped or challenging viewfinders – keyholes, circles, letterboxes, the space between fingers, cylinders, matchboxes etc. Very often you can make use of things in the environment that are themselves viewfinders and that help to place what is seen firmly in place or into context. The most familiar viewfinder is the window frame or window pane. Where a classroom has very big windows, a miniature frame made from paper can be stuck on to put a daunting view or panorama into more manageable proportions.

Other familiar viewfinders:

mirror;
reflections in a bottle;
shiny car bonnet or bumper;
doorway;
gap between houses;
space between trees etc.

A familiar focusing device is the magnifying glass or lens: it clarifies small details and can place familiar things into a new, unfamiliar and exciting context. Viewed through a magnifying glass, woodlice become strange and lumbering monsters, a cluster of television valves becomes a space city, a few twigs a complete forest. Place a familiar object upon an overhead projector and it suddenly fills a wall. Metamorphosis is an important means of stimulating looking and response.

Perception of familiar things can also be sharpened by placing them in an unfamiliar context, such as when they can be felt but not seen, when familiar things are wrapped in paper, black plastic sheeting or cooking foil, or when familiar things

are seen distorted, as in the surface of a shiny spoon, or when objects are seen through reeded or frosted glass. Familiar things transformed challenge children's observation and their imagination, and when the two are harnessed they can produce drawings and responses that go beyond straightforward recording and into personal expression.

Description and talk can also serve as an imaginative focus by placing the looking into a different kind of context. Ask the children to 'see' something on a different scale or from a different point of view: the bird's eye view of your house and garden, a worm's eye view of your shoes, a clump of grass or a group of plants drawn as though it were a jungle.

Changes of scale and of context and meaning all help to transform the routine process of observation and recording and to place them within an expressive context. The child drawing an old boot methodically and carefully is engaged usefully in one kind of drawing. The child who views the surface of an old boot through a tiny viewfinder, like a space traveller hovering over a strange planet, will see and respond to the boot in a different kind of way and produce a different kind of drawing. Both the observed response and the imaginative response are equally valid. There is a close parallel between children's ability to use drawing as a means of personal expression and their competence in using drawing objectively. Children's expressive and imaginative response through drawing is best placed within the context of real experience. The space traveller across the old boot may well achieve something more personal and meaningful than the child whose space travels are determined too much by 'Dr Who', 'Star Wars' and 'Star-Trekkers' of film and television.

Texture, pattern and tone

In order to help children make some kind of sense and order from a busy and complex environment, you can select or isolate certain ele-

Fig. 4.12 Using a window as a viewfinder; pencil (48 × 28 cm). 15-year-old, Axminster School.

Fig. 4.13 Using the space between branches as a viewfinder; ink (40 × 28cm). 15-year-old, Ivybridge School.

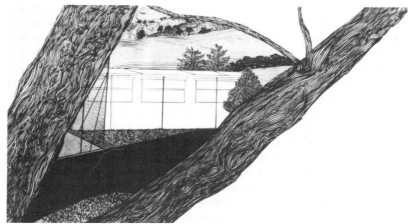

Fig. 4.14 Using a rear view mirror as a viewfinder; tempera colour (50 × 28cm). 15-year-old, Ivybridge School.

Focusing children's attention through the use of familiar viewfinders and focusing devices.

ments of visual forms for particular study. For example, you can ask the children to make rubbings or impressions of all the different kinds of textures and surfaces they can find around the school, or make diagrams of all the patterns they can find in a collection of shells, or record the construction and shape of television aerials in the vicinity of the school.

Children can look for the patterns, tones, surfaces and structures within the man-made and natural world – to develop this visual skill and to provide them with information for their work in design and the crafts. It is very important that this kind of analysis is closely related to a study of the real world, if it is not to be an artificial and academic exercise.

These are some examples of how such studies can be used in other craft and design media:

making studies of fine patterns in leaves and shells to use as designs for work in batik;

taking rubbings from car tyres, bark and iron work to be used as studies for relief patterns in pottery;

making drawings to extract essential information for designs for print-making in a variety of media.

In all analytical drawing the choice of media is crucial and has to be closely related to the element or quality that is being analysed or recorded through the drawing. The children must have a clear understanding of what they are looking for – pattern, texture, colour etc. – and be given media to use that will encourage them to operate in those terms. For example:

Tonal studies may well be 'drawn' in torn newspaper or constructed in strips of black and white paper, or drawn using three different weights of pencil – whichever helps the children to make the analogy most effectively.

Example 1 gives many other examples of the way that media can be matched to the visual qualities that are being investigated.

When you use analytical systems of drawing with younger children in secondary schools, you must relate them closely to real tasks – either of recording aspects of the environment or in design exploration for a particular project. The formal language of space, form, structure, surface and colour can be useful to younger children, but it has little meaning if taught and practised in isolation.

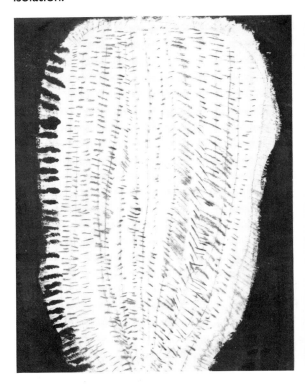

Fig. 4.15   Cactus; charcoal, chalk and ink (58 × 36cm). 11-year-old, Queen Elizabeth School, Crediton.

A selection of analytical drawings in which the children have been assisted in their search to focus upon qualities of surface, pattern and form through the sensible choice of materials which match the qualities they are seeking in the objects and environments they are working from.

Fig. 4.16 Views of our school; pen and ink (30 × 10cm). 13-year-olds, Eggbuckland School, Plymouth.

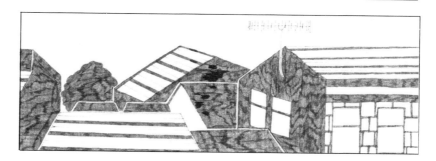

Fig. 4.17 Study of patterns seen through the window; pen and ink (42 × 28cm). 15-year-old, Axminster School.

Fig. 4.18 Interlocking chairs; pen and wash (80 × 59cm). 16-year-old, Dawlish School.

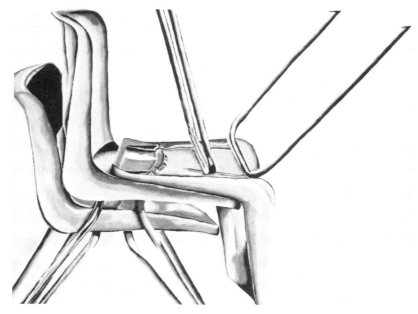

Children become confused unless a close relationship is established between looking, thinking and making. They need to know why they are using drawing to collect information and for what purpose, why they need to make these studies in order to be better equipped to make a print, construct in clay, weave or carve. The relationship between drawing and making is developed in Chapter 7, 'The place of the crafts'.

Drawing for Communication

Drawing can also be used to convey different kinds of information about the world the children live in – as in a diagram or pictorial map, a series of drawings to explain how something works, a form of visual 'story telling' or to record changes and events over a period of time.

This kind of work can be useful in keying children into the constructive use of images, symbols and diagrams. Children all go through a stage where they are fascinated by comics and cartoons, and it is useful to capitalize upon that interest by involving them in problems of how to use the techniques of graphic design to tell simple stories or to explain such things as how they get

from home to school, how they get up in the morning, what they like about school, how they tie their shoe laces etc.

In addition to this kind of source material, there is a whole host of visual communication forms which children are familiar with and which might be used as triggers for different kinds of communication problems and projects for them. These include road signs and symbols, badges, games of all kinds, pop-up books, playing cards, picture puzzles and diagrammatic conventions of various kinds. It is a genuine challenge to children to involve them in problems of communicating information and ideas without using words, in order that they can learn something from the techniques and language of the information media as well as be entertained by it.

Children do absorb at an early age a whole vocabulary of image and symbol association that enables them to 'read' the messages conveyed through the communications media. It is a vocabulary that is rarely tapped and used by teachers. Example 4 is about some drawing projects in which children are being asked to convey information through the use of images and symbols.

Drawings used to convey information, both about familiar events and possessions and also as a means to invent alternatives to familiar experiences.

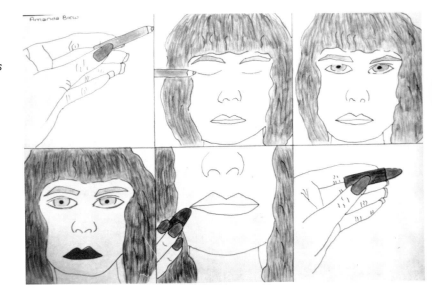

Fig. 4.19 How to apply make-up; felt pens (38 × 27 cm). 14-year-old, Tavistock School.

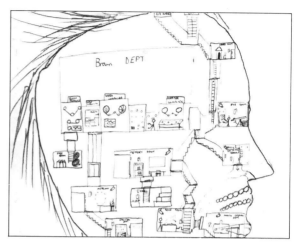

Fig. 4.20   My favourite possessions; pencil (36 × 48cm). 11-year-old, King Edward VIth School, Totnes.

Fig. 4.21   Factory inside my head; pencil (45 × 30cm). 11-year-old, Plymstock School.

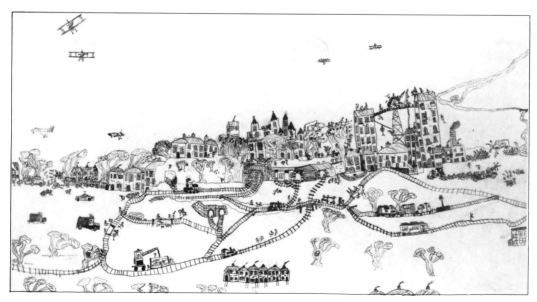

Fig. 4.22   View of Exeter from the classroom window (with additions and embellishments); pencil (58 × 36cm). 12-year-old, Exwick Middle School, Exeter.

Drawing as a Means of Personal Expression

Some techniques that can be used to help children towards using drawing and painting as a means of personal expression have already been described in Chapter 3, 'Teaching strategies and resources'.

Children will use drawing expressively when they are confronted with drawing tasks that require them to move beyond simple description or the straightforward business of conveying information. As with all kinds of drawing, their response will largely be determined by the context within which you place the drawing task. It is one thing to be asked to draw what you look like, but quite another to be asked to draw what is going on inside your head. It is one thing to be asked to draw what you look like now, but quite another to be asked to draw yourself as you would like to look, or as others see you.

Although this kind of drawing may begin with the desire to record and understand the appearance and structure of familiar things, the children's perceptions will inevitably be coloured by the associations, ideas and images evoked by the physical experience of looking and engaging with real things. Children will draw with more feeling when the source material has meaning for them over and above its appearance. 11-year-olds enjoy drawing things that are personal to them – their possessions, things they have collected, their favourite food, themselves and familiar things that are unusually or intriguingly presented to them. 15-year-olds taken to draw at the site of a derelict factory, or an impoverished part of town, will respond to the quality of that environment as well as its appearance.

One way to encourage children to draw expressively is to choose subject matter that has special meaning for them, another is to encourage them to be inventive. At a literal level children can describe how they get from home to school through a series of drawings, but they can also make invented journeys, through a strange landscape, into their own bodies, into the future etc. The act of transforming familiar things into strange things can both challenge and stimulate children, and frequently their best imagining is based upon their trying to find ways to make a metamorphosis from one form into another. They will do this with more assurance if they first observe the familiar object very closely, be it their thumb, their own shoe, their own features etc. (See example 3.) Children can only be truly inventive where their 'imagining' is based upon experience or knowledge.

You can reinforce the observation of familiar things and events to encourage an expressive response using different kinds of stimulus. The drawings made by 11-year-olds in response to a walk through a small copse near their school were expressively focused by poems and prose describing the feelings evoked by woodland and passages of music that were descriptive and pastoral. In the walk through the wood that followed upon the music and readings, the children were encouraged to try to find ways to make their drawings describe the mood and quality of what they saw as well as its appearance.

The task of making a self portrait by a class of 14-year-olds was expressively focused by turning a routine exercise into an amusing one – the children were asked to pull as strange or as funny a face as possible, and these were photographed so that they had photographs of their 'funny faces' as well as their reflections in mirrors to use as source material (figure 4.25).

These techniques are especially useful when dealing with the kind of tasks which children have to repeat, especially in preparation for some examination papers – drawings of portraits, life drawings of the figure, drawings of those familiar and everyday objects that are part of the still-life tradition. You can find ways to prevent these necessary exercises from becoming repetitive and mechanical through using a variety of ploys to regenerate children's response to making the drawing and to encourage them to draw more freely and expressively. You can also use works of art to reinforce children's response to familiar things and environments, and this is dealt with in more detail in Chapter 6, 'Using works of art'.

Two expressive drawings based upon experiences familiar to the children and reinforced through story telling or the use of supporting prose and poetry.

Fig. 4.23   Memories of a dream; pen and ink (42 × 29cm). 11-year-old, Teignmouth High School.

Fig. 4.24   Windy day; pencil (40 × 28cm). 11-year-old, Axminster School.

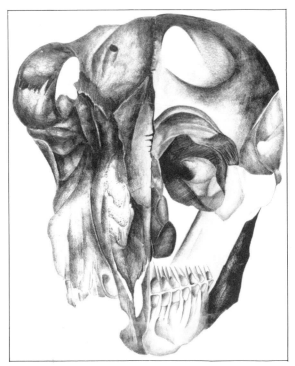

Fig. 4.25   Funny faces; charcoal and chalk (41 × 60cm). 14-year-olds, Priory High School, Exeter.

Fig. 4.26   The skull becomes alive; pencil (20 × 26cm). 15-year-old, Audley park School, Torquay.

Using photography to try to generate fresh interest and stimulus within the convention of portrait drawing. This project began with a 'funny faces' competition. The teacher photographed each child's attempt to distort their own faces, and the children then used these photographs in conjunction with observation of themselves in mirrors to make a drawing of their own 'funny face'.

Older children in secondary schools using drawing as a means to explore ideas and images that have personal meaning and significance to them. In these art departments, the students have been given sufficient confidence and competence in their drawing to be able to use these skills to make very personal statements about their particular view of some aspect of their own social environment.

Fig. 4.27   Cripple man; pen and ink (28 × 40cm). 16-year-old, Dawlish School.

EXAMPLE 1

Using line to explore surface

Robert Clement

A drawing programme for 10/13-year-olds. A series of drawing projects designed to help children to use a variety of drawing media in pursuit of different ways to represent surface. The programme consists of four sections which may be used independently as separate projects or in various combinations to make a sequence of work (see pages 113–14).

---

1 Surface patterns
2 Smooth to rough
3 Lines that follow surfaces
4 Metamorphosis

This programme of work will last for about one term if you are working to the traditional pattern of one afternoon of work in art in each week. Although you can take any one of the sections within this programme and use them in isolation, it is better to try to use them in association or in sequence as they have been designed to develop one from the other. If you wish to do a shorter version of this programme use the following pattern:

Section 1
Section 2 OR Section 3
Section 4 (optional)

Surface patterns   The class can either work through both parts of this section or can be divided into two groups – one group to work on Part A and the other on Part B.

     Initial talk and discussions to be related to a small display of objects with different kinds of surfaces, rubbings taken from them and photographs of larger scale surfaces with interesting patterns.

     Children to try to identify which rubbings have been taken from which surfaces.

     Demonstration of rubbing techniques with emphasis upon need to take impressions carefully and evenly to obtain

EXAMPLE 1

good results. Demonstration of difference between negative and positive rubbings:

Negative with black crayons on white paper or tracing paper. Positive with candles or white crayons on white paper washed over with black ink to obtain negative impression.

A   (i) Children to be given 10 cm squares of paper in order to concentrate selection and care. Work in the environment taking rubbings from natural surfaces:

trees
plants
stones   Emphasis upon looking for
shells   variations within the form,
etc.   e.g. How many patterns can you
find in one tree?

(ii) Class discussion to sort out and arrange rubbings in sequence:

Positive rubbings arranged in order from light to dark.
Negative rubbings to be arranged in order from rough to smooth.
Positive rubbings displayed against white paper.
Negative rubbings against black paper.

(iii) Class to be given good selection of pebbles, shells, bones and pieces of bark. Detailed discussions about differences between surfaces. Children to try to match the objects with the different rubbings in the display.

Are the patterns regular or random?
Are the lines close together or far apart?
Are the lines heavy or light?
Are patterns made up of speckles, dots, curves, splodges, straight lines, wiggly lines etc?

(iv) Children to experiment with HB/2B/3B pencils to see how many shades and different kinds of lines they can make holding and using the pencils in different kinds of ways. Try to match the patterns and marks made with the pencils to some of the different patterns in the collection of rubbings.

(v) Each child to choose one natural object with an interesting or complicated surface and – using magnifying glasses to help close and detailed observations – to draw the surface of the object as carefully and accurately as possible.

(vi) Display objects, rubbings and drawings together. Compare and discuss.

B (i) Children to be given 10 cm squares of paper in order to concentrate selection and care. Work in the environment taking rubbings from man-made surfaces:

buildings
furniture
cars   } Emphasis upon looking
everyday objects   for subtle variations
etc.   in pattern.

(ii) Class discussion to sort out and arrange rubbings in sequence:

Positive rubbings arranged in order from light to dark.
Negative rubbings arranged in order from regular to irregular.
Positive rubbings displayed against white paper.
Negative rubbings displayed against black paper.

(iii) Fill collections of jars and bottles with a variety of materials and man-made objects:

torn paper
string
wool
pins or nails
straws
marbles
pasta
spills
coarse fabrics (netting and hessian)
etc.

Organize competition to see which child can produce the most interesting patterns inside a bottle or jar.

(iv) Children to be given small paper viewfinders (approximately 5 cm^2) and asked to use them to select a surface pattern inside the bottles/jars that

EXAMPLE I

they particularly like. (Viewfinders to be Sellotaped into place after selection.)

Class discussion to find out parallels between rubbings made from man-made objects and collections of surface patterns.

Are the patterns regular or random?
Are the lines close together or far apart?
Are the lines delicate and faint or strong and heavy?
Are the lines straight, curved, wiggly etc?

(v) Children to experiment with different mark-making media to see what kinds of lines they make on different kinds of paper:

pencil
steel pen   white cartridge
Biro   newsprint
felt pen   on   tracing paper
black crayon   tissue paper
charcoal

(vi) Children to choose which kind of line would be best to use to draw the pattern they can see in their glass container, or what combination of lines might be needed.

Careful observation and drawing of patterns.

(vii) Display drawings, patterns and rubbings together. Discuss.

Smooth to rough

(i) Make display of collection of objects with different kinds of surfaces:

scrubbing brush, sandpaper, scourer, wire netting, fabric materials (net, gauze, hessian, scrim, velvet, silk etc.), sponge, cotton wool, nylon, wallpapers, string, shoes, plastics, eroded metal etc.

Arrange in order from rough to smooth against a ground of different textured papers (wallpapers, corrugated, tracing, blotting etc.).

(ii) Each child to have A2 sheet grey paper divided into 20 squares. Children to experiment with the following media to try to make 20 different kinds of surface by using materials in different kinds of combinations – by applying with different kinds of movements – soft, hard, using edge or point etc. and by drawing over media with different kinds of media:

white and black powder paint
white and black tempera (block or liquid)
charcoal
black ink
white and black crayon
hard and soft pencils
white chalk

(iii) Children to work in pairs – one to be blindfolded and the other to hand to his partner different objects in turn and to write down six words the blindfolded child can use to describe the 'feel' of each object, e.g.

close
sharp
bristly
furry
soft
smooth
nasty
rippling
etc.

Some preliminary language work will be necessary and desirable.

Children to compare groups of words used to describe objects with the experimental surfaces they have made. Do some surfaces match the groups of words? Do the surfaces that match the groups of words look like the objects those words describe?

(iv) Each child to make detailed drawing of three different objects to describe the surface of the object. To choose one rough, one smooth and one in between.
Children to mount drawing in rough/smooth sequence on one sheet of paper.

(v) Discuss.

(vi) Select building or group of buildings in the vicinity of the school that possess a variety of surfaces, e.g.

row of terraced houses
churchyard
eroded or battered buildings
barns or outbuildings
factory
garden huts or sheds
etc.

EXAMPLE 1

Children to make drawings and notes on site.

To use experimental surface charts to identify qualities and effects in the buildings observed.

Words to describe qualities of surface and appearance of buildings.

Outline drawings of whole group of buildings.

Detailed notes on part of buildings.

Experimental studies with different media to recreate surface qualities of buildings.

(vii) Drawings to be reconstructed and developed in classroom. If groups of buildings are particularly complex then children to work in small groups on one large drawing or a series of drawings to be linked and mounted together.

(viii) Display and discuss.

Lines that follow surfaces

(i) Observation and discussion about contour maps – how they work and on what principle.

Simple drawing exercises. Make a contour map of:

your knuckle
your friend's nose
a pebble
etc.

(ii) Each child to make small template of a simple irregular shape from cardboard. Use the template to reproduce six repeated shapes on one piece of paper.

Children to be asked to fill the shape with linear patterns that grow like contour maps, or the ripples in a pond to fill the shape.

Children to use a different drawing medium for each of the six shapes, e.g. pencil, crayon, Biro, felt pen, charcoal, chalk.

In addition to filling the shape with a linear and growing pattern, the children should be asked to use a *variation in the quality of line* as the contours grow and change inside the shape, e.g. lines to grow or change from:

hard to soft
light to dark
strong to delicate
straight to wobbly
etc.

(iii) Careful observation to be made of some of the following or any objects or forms where the direction and quality of line reveals the shape and structure of the form:

bark
driftwood
feathers
ribbed shells
ball of string
loose hessian
etc.

Comparisons to be made between objects and 'contour' drawings to identify similar effects or patterns. Children to make careful drawings of one of these objects from close observation.

(iv) Experiments with different media of drawing through or 'resist' drawing techniques, e.g. scratching through black crayon, indian ink, paint etc., using sharp pencils, end of paint brush, sharp tools etc.

(v) Observation and discussion about reproductions of paintings and drawings where line is used to follow or 'describe' the form beneath as in Van Gogh, Japanese woodcuts, Bewick's woodcuts, Munch etc.

Observation and discussion about collection of photographs of form revealed by linear patterns across the surface as in:

ploughed fields
light through venetian blinds
striped clothes
zebras
hair and fur of animals
etc.

(vi) Set up drawing groups for children to work from. Preliminary discussions about choice and range of media to be used. Possible choice of subjects:

Child in striped pyjamas lying under a striped sheet.
Striped cat sitting on a patterned cushion.
Girl with elaborate hair-do.
Guinea pigs on straw.
Old lady with wrinkled face.
(On sunny days) Someone in white dress or sweater sitting in front of a window with venetian blinds etc.

EXAMPLE 2

EXAMPLE 2

Shoe questionnaire

John Broomhead   *Head of Art Department, Great Torrington School*

A written questionnaire used as the starting point for a project on shoes. The questionnaire was designed both to encourage children to observe their shoes more closely and to begin to consider different aspects and functions of their shoes.

Questionnaire

?
SHOES

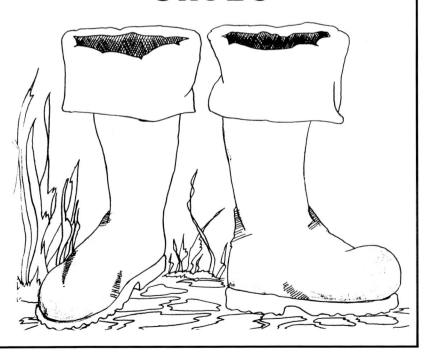

Answer the questions below

about the shoes you are wearing now.

1 What size shoe do you take? _____

2 Exactly what colour are your shoes? _____

3 Are the laces lighter, darker or the same as the rest of your shoe? _____

4 If you have no laces, how are your shoes kept on? _____

5 Can you describe the pattern on the sole of your shoe? _____

6 How are the uppers attached to the bottoms? _____

7 What are your shoes made of? _____

8 Describe in detail any patterns on your shoe. _____ _____

9 Do your shoes come above or below your ankle? _____

10 Have your shoes got low or high heels? _____

11 If your heels are high, how high? _____

12 Do your shoes have any particular job to perform? _____ _____

13 How worn are your shoes? _____

14 When did you buy them? _____

15 Where did you buy them? _____

16 Do you like them? Give reasons. _____ _____

17 Are they comfortable? _____

18 Give reasons for your answer above. _____

19 Are your shoes fashionable? _____

20 Do your shoes smell? _____

21 If they do, why? _____

22 Describe how your shoes feel to the touch. _____ _____

23 Do your friends like your shoes? _____

24 Do you look after your shoes? _____

25 What do you clean them with? _____

26 How often do you clean them? _____

27 Do you think your shoes are happy or unhappy? _____

28 Do your shoes let in the wet? _____

29 Do your shoes keep your feet warm? _____

30 If you could go out and buy a new pair of shoes *now*, what would they be like? _____

EXAMPLE 3

EXAMPLE 3

Myself

Stephen Disbrey   *Art and Craft Co-ordinator, Lower School, Paignton College*

A drawing project for first-year children. Used as the first piece of work when the children enter this school both as a means to get to know the children quickly and to focus the children's looking through careful observation of different aspects of themselves.

???MYSELF

This discovery project is called 'Myself', and, during the next few weeks, you are going to examine yourself and have the opportunity of taking a closer look at each other.

Nearly all the people that we meet look very much alike. Each has a nose, two eyes, a mouth, hair; most of them have the same colour of skin; their clothes are similar. How then do we recognize them? Why do we but rarely mistake one person for another?

A possible answer to these questions is that we identify people by the features that make them different from others, such as colour and length of hair, size, shape, complexion and age. Presumably we notice these things unconsciously because we rarely say to ourselves, 'What a straight nose he has' or 'Her two front teeth are uneven'.

In fact, when we are asked to describe people, we often discover that we can recall little of their appearances. Our descriptions may refer instead to the way they talk and dress, what they say, their irritating mannerisms, or how they behave.

Our descriptions, therefore, are often based on our assessment of them, on whether we like them or not. These assessments are individual things. A mannerism found irritating by one person will be ignored by another; features found beautiful by some will be thought ugly by others. Because of this it is unlikely that any two people will describe a person in the same way. The characteristics they select will vary according to what they think of the person and their own likes and dislikes.

Answer the questionnaire called 'Myself'.

Instructions Look about the room. You will see a number of activity areas. You can decide which you wish to use for a particular piece of work.

Remember only four people can use an area at the same time. If you wish to use an area which is full, do a different activity and return to it later.

Only one activity may be done at a time and this should be completed. You may not begin another activity until you have shown your finished work to the class teacher and have cleaned up the area.

You can decide the order in which you explore the following:

Hands Make a plan of your hand in your book, front and back. You can draw, paint or print this hand. Be as accurate as possible. Use your questionnaire to help you. Collect photos of the hand for next week.

Now do some of these activities:

Make a collage (stuck down picture) of the photographs you have collected. Arrange them carefully first.

Print your palms and fingers.

Paint or draw your hand holding an object chosen from those in the room.

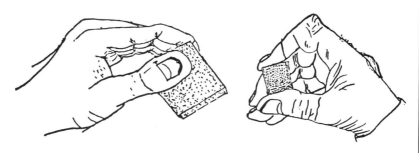

EXAMPLE 3

Print your finger prints. Are they the same as other people's?

Look at your hand using a magnifying glass. Record what you see.

Using Plasticine, make a ball, a cylinder and a cube. Squeeze and push your fingers and knuckles into them. Look at the shapes you make. Can you record them in any way?

Roll out a small slab of Plasticine. Can you make your own private marker using only your hands, nails and fingers?

How will you record this?

Collect together your work. Is it neat and tidy? Can you place any of it on your body plan? Put the rest in your workbook or body folder.

As others see me

Work in pairs. Try to choose someone you know. Ask your friend as many questions as you can think of on how they view you. Make them be honest. Try to make a complete view of your friend as you see him/her. Make pictures of them from as many different angles as possible. They have probably never seen themselves from the back, the floor or the sides. Observe and record them as accurately as possible. Use their questionnaire to help you. Can you make a cartoon picture of them? Do you think of a particular object or situation when you think of them? Do they have any features that stick out more than others?

What does their hair look like from the back? Make a drawing using lines drawn with a fine nibbed felt tip pen.

Draw your friend's ear on a small piece of paper, they will be pleased to see what it looks like!

Collect together your work. Is it neat and tidy? Have you cleared up your work area?

From magazines and newspapers select photographs of three members of the opposite sex whom you consider to be attractive or beautiful. Stick the photographs into your notebook and underneath each one give the reasons why the person appeals to you.

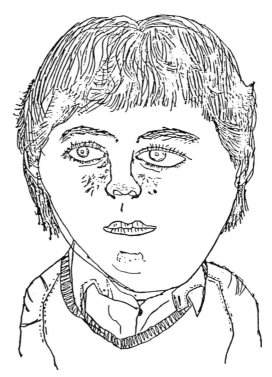

Head   Using a mirror and your questionnaire to help you, make a life-size self portrait of your head. Ask the teacher to show you famous artists' self portraits. You decide how to make it.
Now do some of these activities:

EXAMPLE 3

Use a projector and work with a friend. Draw round each other's shadow, frontwards and sideways. Use these drawings to make a silhouette.

Can you use the template any other ways? Making an overlapping pattern of shapes, or lines? Or printing the shape into a pattern?

Can you use the shapes of single features, eye, nose, ear or lips to make patterns? Observe and record them carefully first. Design a book cover or piece of wrapping paper using printed features.

Make a face shape. (Look at the questionnaire – choose one of the shapes suggested there.) Make and cut out ears, eyebrows, eyelashes, nose and lips and arrange them in an unusual way on the face shape. Stick them down.

Look at the teacher's book on portraits by Picasso and see how he does them.

Use grey paper, chalk/charcoal and shine a spotlight on your friend's face. Block in the light and dark areas on the correct face shape.

Will your portrait fit on your body plan? Is your work tidy and clean? Tidy up your work area.

Body Working with your friend, do four drawings in different positions. Any interesting ones will do – kneeling, sitting, stretching, crouching. Try to use different markers – felt, chalk, charcoal, pencil, pastel. You choose. Which do you prefer?

Choose your favourite drawing. Can you make a line pattern from it overlapping the shapes?

Can you make a cartoon filling in different positions and adding a story and speech?

Put the clothes you are wearing now on your body plan. Look at them carefully.

Choose one of Spike Milligan's goblin poems. Read it and draw the character. Think about the shape of the body. Ask the teacher to show you the illustration from the book when you have finished.

Feet Do some prints of the foot. Make sure you wash them afterwards! Compare your feet with others, how are yours different?

Look at your foot carefully. Draw it. Draw your friend's foot from the side. Does it look like yours?

Cut out a template of your foot. Make a card from it. Can you make it happy, sad, angry, sleepy, by altering its toes? Can you develop a funny character? What is its name? Does it smell? Where does it live?

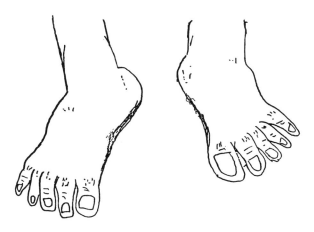

EXAMPLE 4

EXAMPLE 4

Graphic communication worksheets

Peter Riches   *Head of Creative Studies Department, Eggbuckland
School, Plymouth*

Two worksheets designed to encourage children to use signs and
symbols to tell stories and explore different aspects of familiar
things (see page 122).

Picture – Story
Plan a series of simple drawings to describe the sequence of
movements made in *one* of the following situations:

1 *The accident*
2 *Waking up*
3 *Eating an ice cream or a lollipop*

Use any available drawing media – Biro/pencil/felt pen.
Keep the pattern of tone-lights/darks consistent over the
eight frames.

NORMAL VIEW | BIRDSEYE | OVERHEAD | WORMSEYE

Using the above example to guide you, develop *one* of the
following themes in its natural setting:

1 *My house*
2 *My favourite meal*
3 *The family car*
4 *A personal object*

Normal View	Birdseye
Overhead	Wormseye

You should develop your chosen theme in the form of
drawings – line and shading – within the spaces. Please use
any media available – pen/pencil/felts.

5 PAINTING AS AN EXTENSION OF DRAWING

For children to paint with confidence they have to be taught how to use both colour and pigment and to be given some understanding of the relationship between drawing and painting.

Many children at the age of eleven will arrive at their secondary school having done little painting since their first couple of years of schooling. Many will view painting as a means of colouring in drawings – and will have been frustrated by the number of times they have ruined a perfectly good drawing by trying to paint over it!

Painting has to be seen as an extension of drawing and not as the second stage where you apply colour to a drawing. The choice of subject matter is also crucial to giving children confidence in their approach to making a painting. You need to be much more selective in the use of content and source material as a support to the teaching of painting than you do when embarking upon drawing with children. In addition to teaching children about colour – how to see it and how to use it – there is a real need to match their knowledge of colour to content they can handle, to make a proper marriage between content and form. It is also valuable to make consistent use of the work of other painters in support of the children's own work.

Colour and Pigment

Children need to be taught about colour – how it works and how it may be differently applied. There is a tendency amongst some teachers to overelaborate the teaching of colour theory, reflecting back perhaps to their own art school training. Children respond better to the more direct teaching of colour, where there is a clear link between making colour and using it. It is for

this reason that the making of the standard colour wheel is a fairly pointless exercise. It may take up four whole lessons to put together, and in the end the children are still unlikely to be able to relate the theory to the practice of using colour in a picture. This kind of exercise is also misleading in that it frequently separates making colour from using pigment.

Understanding of colour is best taught through a combination of demonstration, and playing colour games. (See pictures 1 and 2 in the colour section.)

Demonstration

Range and quality of colour can easily be demonstrated to children in a variety of ways. You can use an overhead projector and a combination of coloured Cellophanes and gelatines to demonstrate quickly to children the basic colour changes between primary and secondary colour. Use colour source material from colour supplements and magazines to display for children the subtle range of colour that can be achieved through various kinds of mixing and overpainting. Use colour charts produced by paint manufacturers, the material swatches to be found in most tailor's shops etc. Display source material of this kind together with real evidence of colour in natural and man-made forms, as in the use of the conventional colour table. See pages 78–82 for more information about how the source material may be ordered and arranged in such a way as to underline its meaning.

Games

Children will learn most about colour and more quickly when they explore colour properties in small groups, each group within the class comparing and contrasting their findings with those of other groups. These preliminary investigations are very simple: how colours mix, how to make them change, matching colours, seeing how colours vary depending upon ground and pigment etc. It is more productive to set a group a variety of tasks and then to compare the results, than to require every child to work their way through a whole series of exercises. The table overleaf shows a range of games, and the materials needed to play them, with examples from the red/pink/orange/purple range of colour.

Example 1 gives a variety of further colour explorations children might undertake as part of their first-year course.

If children are to learn how to make and use colour effectively, you need to give them the right palette and media to use. For the beginnings of work in colour, there is no doubt that powder colours are the most effective medium. Although the Redimix colours can provide greater density and range of weight, because they are 'ready mixed' in tubes, younger children tend to use them too much like toothpaste! The very fact that powder colours have to be mixed with water before they work at all encourages the children to work with different densities of paint. The difference between using powder colours and Redimix colours is rather like the difference between learning to play the piano and the violin. The notes on the piano are already there – all you have to do is to learn how to play them in the right sequence. Notes on the violin have to be made by the performer.

The basic palette should be white, yellow, vermilion, crimson, ultramarine and black. As the children gain more experience, then both cobalt and Prussian blue might be added to extend the range. Once the children have mastered the basic skills of colour-making and using paint in powder colours, you can gradually introduce Redimix colours, gouache etc. as they begin to need a more sophisticated range of media to match the more demanding content of their work.

In the same way as in the teaching of drawing you can encourage children to experiment with and practise different ways of making marks and combining different media, so in the teaching of painting it is valuable to pursue with the children the variety of ways that paint may be applied and used. As they learn about colour, you need to provide activities and experiments to help them to see and enjoy the plasticity of pigment – how it may be differently applied even with a paint-brush, how it may be used transparently and opaquely, how it works when mixed with other media etc. All this experimental and exploratory use of colour should be directly related to using colour for a specific task, so that there is a clear link between learning about colour and using it. For example, you can follow up an investigation into the range of colours between cream and orange with direct paintings from simple groups of such fruits as bananas, lemons, oranges and peaches set against a cream or white ground. Some of the preliminary work on how to apply paint differently is then used to match the different surface textures of these fruits. (See also the jar of feathers, picture 3 in the colour section.)

The Transition from Drawing to Painting

It is a comparatively simple task to teach children about colour and how to apply colour in making colour studies or paintings from direct observation of natural and man-made forms. It is more difficult to establish a proper relationship between drawing an image and painting it. By the time they are ten or eleven, many children tend to view painting as being a second stage to drawing – first you draw the image and then you colour it in with paint! This frequently leads to much frustration, as most children at this stage can draw with some precision but find it difficult to add the paint to the drawn image without ruining it. This is often because there is a mismatch between the scale of the drawing and that needed for a painting, and because the children do not possess the skill or experience to use paint with the same precision as they can draw. It

Resources	Activities
Overhead projector Gelatine and Cellophane sheets Slide projector Colour slides Windows Cellophanes, coloured tissues, sweet papers etc. Colour spectacles, viewfinders with colour inserts, pieces of coloured glass, colour paddles and prisms etc.	Making and observing colour change. Mixing colours on an overhead projector by placing different gelatines and Cellophanes over each other. Projecting colour slides over different objects and parts of the room. Looking at familiar things through coloured spectacles. Making colour charts and patterns on windows using tissue papers and other transparent materials.
Powder colour (vermilion), water and different coloured papers. Powder colour – vermilion, yellow, ultramarine, white. Powder colour – vermilion, crimson, ultramarine, white, yellow and black.	Experimenting to see how many colours you can make with one colour by using different amounts of water and by painting over different coloured papers. How many colours can you make with vermilion plus one other colour? How many shades can you make between one and the other? How many colours can you make using vermilion mixed with varying quantities of two other colours, e.g. vermilion plus white plus yellow, or vermilion plus crimson plus ultramarine, or vermilion plus ultramarine plus black, etc?
Selection of colour charts. Natural and man-made objects. Colour range: reds/pinks/oranges/purples.	Arrange and display colour charts divided into four main groups: oranges, pinks, browns and purples. Oral colour mixing – comparing colours made with colours in display. Work in pairs – mixing and matching colours – children to challenge each other to match particular colours. Colour mixing from memory – choose an object and match its colour unseen etc.

Small display groups – selection of coloured papers against which are displayed natural and man-made forms.
One group each of papers and objects which are red, pink, orange or purple dominated.
	Using viewfinders, select small part of one group. Paint the colours and shapes you can see –
	    from memory,
	    from observation.
	Introduce use of collage in association with painting.
	Project colour slides over group and observe changes in colour. Paint the change that takes place etc.

is for this reason that some care has to be taken in the choice of subject matter or content when you are looking for ways to follow up the familiar colour exercises described above.

You may choose to make a clear distinction between collecting information by making colour studies and drawings, and using these in a painting. This is particularly useful when children are working from the environment and where their initial studies will be followed up by working directly in paint on a much larger scale. Children learn a great deal about painting by being required to paint directly – to draw with paint and to add colour and detail entirely through the application of pigment. It is also a most useful way of showing the children that paint is a very flexible medium – that it doesn't matter if mistakes are made in the early stages because they can be painted out. Figures 5.1 and 5.2 show examples of children's use of direct painting methods, where they have followed up initial studies with larger scale paintings.

Another way into painting is to establish a logical link between drawing and painting by asking the children to make a series of studies that lead them through the use of different media into making a painting. With younger children these studies might be a series of drawings from the same source material. For example, as in figure 5.3, they might begin by making studies of a shoe in pencil (looking for shape and pattern), move on to tonal studies in other media such as charcoal and chalk, and then to making colour studies in crayons and pastels before attempting a painting of the most interesting part of their shoes.

Two good examples of the free use of pigment. This is more common in younger children who are less inhibited about drawing with paint and make less separation between drawing and painting. Older children frequently have to be set direct painting problems to overcome their tendency to draw elaborately before starting to use colour.

Fig. 5.1   Winter landscape; powder colour (30 × 42 cm). 9-year-old, Thornburt Primary School, Plymouth.

Fig. 5.2   Winter trees; tempera (40 × 60 cm). 15-year-old, South Molton School.

147

Fig. 5.3 Shoe studies;
pencil, charcoal, chalks and
crayons. 10-year-old, Manor
Junior School, Ivybridge.
*Leading from drawing towards
the use of colour and painting:
top left – shoe drawn in line
from memory; top right – shoe
drawn from observation in
pencil and attempting to render
tone; bottom right – first colour
study of shoe using pencil,
charcoal and crayons; bottom
left – detailed colour study of
part of shoe using full range of
materials.*

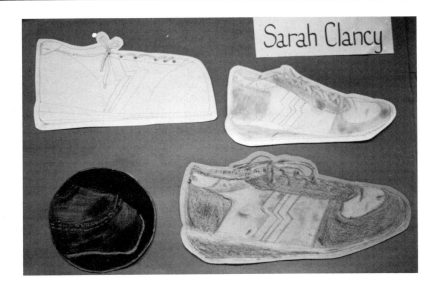

The sequence from drawing in line to drawing in tone to drawing with colour, before moving on to making a painting, is particularly helpful in the early years of secondary schooling, because it capitalizes upon the greater confidence that children have in their drawing.

Intermediate studies are a valuable support to children's painting and, even when working from comparatively simple source material, can help children to approach a painting with more confidence. The choice of media for these studies will obviously vary depending upon the subject matter – and may range from making simple colour charts to tonal studies to detailed colour studies in a variety of media. Figures 5.4 to 5.7 show examples of intermediate studies for paintings in a variety of media and for different kinds of content. (See also Picture 4 in the colour section.)

If children are given experience of a variety of ways into painting, and are helped to see that the way they approach a painting is considerably influenced by the subject matter, they are more likely to face with confidence those more complex painting tasks they will need and want to work on in their later years in the school.

Content and Sequence

The general principles of developing sequence and structure in the teaching of art apply particularly to the teaching of painting, especially in the first two years of secondary schooling. In these early years it is essential to match the painting task carefully to the colour and handling skills that have been taught. It makes little sense to jump from some elementary work in, say, the difference between warm and cool colours to asking the children to paint imaginary landscapes which are either 'hot or cold'. Children in this age range find it very difficult to draw from recall or memory, let alone to recall the subtleties of colour or to invent them to match an 'imaginative' theme.

Because of the complexities of constructing a painting, it is rarely satisfactory to ask children to paint as a one-off activity. It is more sensible to set aside something like a half-term unit of five or six sessions to take the children through a series of activities that will give them a combination of handling and colour skills and the opportunity to apply these skills directly in response to simple painting tasks. Examples 1 and 2 both illustrate

Fig. 5.4   Dartmoor study;
pen and wash (30 × 25cm).
11-year-old, Woodfield
Junior School, Plymouth.

Fig. 5.5   School playing
fields; chalk, charcoal and
pastels (30 × 40cm).
12-year-old, Priory High
School, Exeter.

*Intermediate studies in
preparation for painting.
Using different materials in
preliminary studies to help
children begin to see some of
the possibilities within the
subject matter for developing
paintings from the same
source material. The
materials used help them to
focus upon those colour and
surface qualities that are an
important part of painting.*

Fig. 5.6 View from window; pencil and crayons (32 × 27cm). 12-year-old, Axminster School.

Fig. 5.7 Study for a skull; tempera and collage (42 × 29cm). 11-year-old, Grenville College.

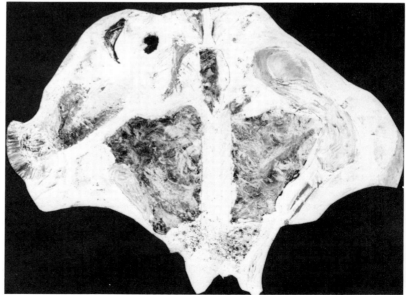

how such a sequence might be established, and how there might be a gradual build up of colour skills related to more demanding painting tasks. In both programmes there is an emphasis on direct experience of colour as the most useful way to help children in their painting. Unless children are given this kind of grounding it is unlikely that they will be able to tackle the more demanding, complex and personal themes that become more appropriate later in the school.

The preparation, thinking and organization that go into the making of a painting can be logically taught, especially when the process is laid alongside and compared with the way that artists work. Example 3 illustrates the way that a group of 10/11-year-olds were encouraged to research and build up information for a painting of activities in their own playground, in direct comparison with the working method of an artist and a particular work.

There is no doubt that children learn a great deal about painting by looking at other paintings. Even in reproduction, the study of the work of other artists can provide children with valuable information about how a painting is put together, how paint is used, how attention and focus are achieved etc. Chapter 6 'Using works of art' pursues some of these possibilities.

Pictures 5 to 8 on pages 3 and 4 of the colour section following page 152 were undertaken by a group of fifth year students working for four days on a residential art workshop in Exmouth.

Their first day was spent in the studio in a variety of drawing exercises, where they were required to work in a variety of media from different kinds of source material.

This was followed by one day drawing for information and in different media using the harbour and beach as their starting point (Figs. 1/6).

These preliminary studies were further developed over two days of studio work (figures 7/13). The work reflects the value in giving older students the opportunity to work intensively in this way and in requiring them to draw and paint directly from experience of the environment.

Working directly from the environment. A selection of paintings which emphasize the value to children of working directly from observation of the environment, where they are faced with the problem and challenge of recording that subtlety of colour and surface that every environment presents (Figs. 5.8–5.11).

Fig. 5.8 Hedge; tempera (42 × 60cm). 15-year-old, Bideford School.

Fig. 5.9   Sidmouth beach;
tempera (58 × 40cm).
15-year-old, Sidmouth
College.

Fig. 5.10   Lyme Regis;
powder colour. 12-year-old,
Axminster School.

Fig. 5.11   Lyme Regis;
powder colour. 12-year-old,
Axminster School.

The pictures on these four pages illustrate points made in Chapter 5 'Painting as an extension of drawing' (see page 144)

Picture 1 (above) Windows and overlapping tissue papers are used to demonstrate basic principles of colour mixing (see page 144). Picture 2 (below) Different coloured papers and pigments are used to explore a range of colour between yellow and red (see pages 144, 146 and 153).

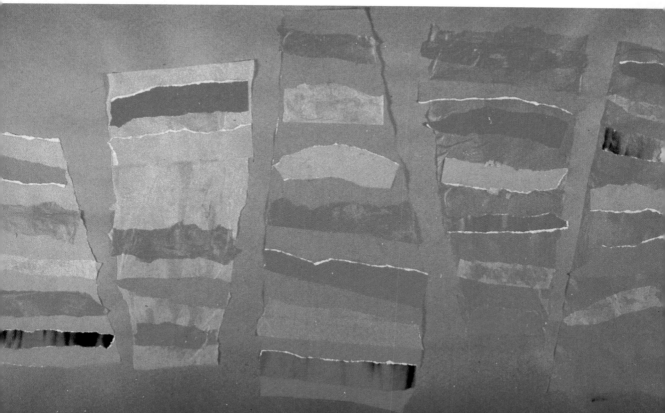

Picture 3 (right) Colour resources. A jar of feathers is used to stimulate observation and talk about subtle differences in texture and colour (see page 145).

Picture 4 (below) Painting of a beach scene by a 12-year-old. This shows how children may be encouraged to use paint in different ways as a result of working from subject matter which tests their handling of pigment (see page 148).

corrugated
metal

Pictures 5, 6, 7 and 8 are by
16-year-olds who attended a
residential workshop at Rolle
College, Exmouth. They were
encouraged to draw and paint
directly from the environment
of Exmouth beach and
harbour. The paintings
illustrate how well children
react to the challenge of using
colour in response to the
experience of colour in the
environment (see page 151).

Preliminary studies: Picture 5
(above) Water colour and
coloured pencils. Picture 6
(left) Water colour and
crayons.

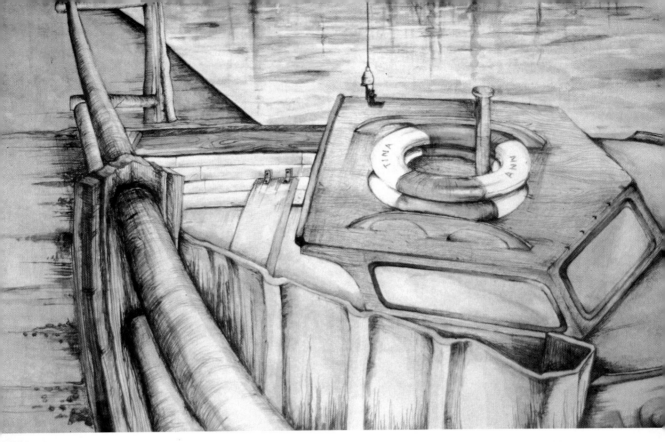

Picture 7 (above) Harbour wall with boat; water colour, tempera and pencil.

Picture 8 (left) Boat under the cliffs; mixed media.

EXAMPLE I

A red programme for first-year children

Robert Clement

1 Display of photographs and reproductions of works of art that are red dominated, plus selection of different coloured papers and materials.
Discussion about these and differences between different reds. When does red become orange or pink or mauve? Discussion about use of 'red' words colloquially, e.g. pillar-box red, scarlet, rouge, red for danger, I saw red etc.

2 Demonstration of how different reds are made by placing tissue papers, Cellophanes and gelatines over each other and using a light source – window or overhead projector.

3 Children play colour-making games – working in pairs and challenging each other to make more reds using combinations of:

red plus yellow;
red plus blue;
red plus white;
red plus black.

4 Children to collect and bring to school a variety of man-made and natural objects – all in different shades between orange/purple and pink/brown.
Colour selection and matching exercises using colours made in previous session and colours in display against objects found.
Oral colour mixing – describe how you might make this or that red.

5 Simple groups of found objects set up against paper and material grounds. Children to observe groups through viewfinders and to select a small part which has interesting shapes and a variety of reds and – after observation and discussion – to paint their chosen part from memory.

6 Children to play colour and pigment games.

EXAMPLE 3

Fig. 5.12 Playground games; pencil and crayons.

Fig. 5.13 Building study; pen and wash.

Working like an artist. *Drawing studies and paintings by 10/11-year-olds who, after studying the painting 'Children's games' by Bruegel, were encouraged to embark upon a painting like an artist – first making preliminary drawings of children's games in their own playground and studies of buildings within the playground, before making their own painting of 'Children's games in my school'. 10/11-year-olds, Ashburton Primary School.*

Fig. 5.14   Building studies; powder colour.

Fig. 5.15   Children's games at Ashburton Primary School; powder colour (35 × 50cm).

EXAMPLE 3

Do you like the picture?

Is it an easy picture to understand?

Can you read the picture, like a story?

If you were making a picture like this, is there anything you would want to be different?

Second session

Looking around the playground

Look for changing shapes of moving groups of children. Do two or three children make more interesting shapes than one child alone?

You can make different shapes in PE with a partner, or in threes, than you can by yourself. You can do this in a drawing too.

Can we sometimes guess what children are playing by the shapes they make? e.g. leapfrog, marbles.

Look at the shapes of the spaces between feet. How many heads are tilted one way or another? How many hands are up in the air? How many children sitting or bending down?

Drawing

In groups, take turns in posing and drawing. Set up a few children in an interesting position that they can keep for five minutes. Make quick drawings with chalk, crayon or charcoal.

Walk round them and decide which is the most interesting view.

Look at the shape of their feet on the floor.

Look at the way arms and legs bend.

Are there any 'windows' through the figures? What shapes are they?

Make as many quick drawings as you can of different groups.

Make your drawings different sizes.

Don't try to do detailed drawings – there won't be time.

You can look at faces and hands more carefully later.

Third session

Looking at school playgrounds and surrounding buildings

Find an interesting part.

Look for corners, paths, different levels, steps, roof shapes, windows, doorways, railings, walls.

Make a working drawing of the place you have chosen, to give you as much information as possible.

You can write about colours and textures on your drawing.

Look at the size of one building against another. How big does a door or window look against a whole house?

Look for the differences between one building and another.

Do the windows look light or dark?

Why do stone walls look different to brick ones?

Fourth session

Making a picture

Look at all the drawings you have made. Do you want to use them all?

Make a little plan of your picture.

If you want the children to be the most important part they will have to be quite big, and will probably overlap the drawing of the buildings. Decide which part of the background you want to see.

Make rough cut-out figures like your drawings and move them round on your picture.

Do they need to be bigger or smaller, closer together or further apart?

Which looks best?

Make your picture. Decide whether it is going to be a painting, collage, pastel, crayon or pen and ink drawing. Choose the right size and sort of paper.

6 USING WORKS OF ART

Evidence of the work of artists, craftsmen and designers, whether in original form or in reproduction, can provide children with very real support to their own studio work. It should be part of every art teacher's armoury to use that mass of evidence that exists in the world of art to help children clue into the various ways the familiar problems of representing and making have been dealt with, both in contemporary art and in that of the past.

George Braque is reputed to have said, 'All art springs from nature and from art.' We can rightly ask the children to seek for their inspiration and information within the natural and man-made world that surrounds us; we can also ensure that in their pursuit of the world of experience they refer to and use that quality and range of seeing that is so evident in the work of other artists.

The use of works of art to generate discussion and appraisal with children, and to feed their own knowledge of ways of seeing and making, has much more meaning for them than the traditional and conventional notion of teaching 'art history'. Many art teachers have consciously rejected the use of works of art with children simply because of their own experiences of being taught the history of art through a sequential and fact collecting routine!

Criticism and Appraisal

The simplest way of engaging children in some kind of appraisal is to give them a selection of prints or reproductions, to ask them to select the one painting they particularly like and to explain and extend upon their choice. You must remember that 'liking' a picture can be as dismissive as 'disliking' it, and that you will need to pursue the question of like and dislike vigorously by, for example, asking them to distinguish between their liking for the content (what story the painting tells) and their liking for the way the artist has used the elements of visual form to put the image together.

As described in Chapter 3, 'Teaching strategies and resources', it is nearly always more productive to engage the children in preliminary discussion amongst themselves and in small groups before trying to generate class discussion about a painting or a group of paintings. One method is to divide the class into six groups and to give each group the same set of postcard reproductions of paintings, asking each group to determine democratically their order of preference. Compare the findings of each group and the qualities they find in the most popular work. A group of 11-year-olds placed Degas' 'L'absinthe' top of their list for the following reasons:

it was realistic;
the colours were harmonious;
it looked old fashioned;
the use of angles to draw your eyes into the picture;
there was a lot of good detail;
it was easy to understand;
they could identify with the characters;
etc.

The selection and choice of those works you present to the children for their appraisal is particularly important. Random choices may be useful to generate discussion in some circumstances, but it is more frequently useful to select a group of works because they lend themselves

Fig. 6.1 Alice (after Modigliani); powder colour (14 × 25cm). 8-year-old, Bridgetown C of E Primary School, Totnes. The children were asked to choose from a large selection of reproductions the one painting they would most like to have in their bedroom. They wrote about why they liked it and then painted their own version for their own room.

Alice Modigliani

I think Alice is sad. I think she has got a sad look on her face. Her eyes are slanted and they are brown. Her dress is pale blue and if I had this picture I would put it in my bedroom. My bedroom is white. I think she looks sad because she has a pursed up mouth. She is thinking very hard about something.

Dunstan Ferris Age 8

Fig. 6.3(a)   A soul called Ida (after Fig. 6.3(b); tempera (50 × 38cm). 15-year-old, Audley Park School, Torquay.

These paintings were in response to written descriptions of paintings made by the children themselves. Two parallel classes undertook an appraisal and description of a favourite painting. The two classes exchanged written descriptions and the children then made paintings based upon these descriptions.

Fig. 6.3(b)   'Into the world there came a soul called Ida', oil on canvas, 1929–30 by Ivan Albright (140 × 118cm) from the collection of The Art Institute of Chicago. © The Art Institute of Chicago. All Rights Reserved.

Fig. 6.4   After 'The card players' by Paul Cézanne; tempera (50 × 38cm). 15-year-old, Audley Park School, Torquay.

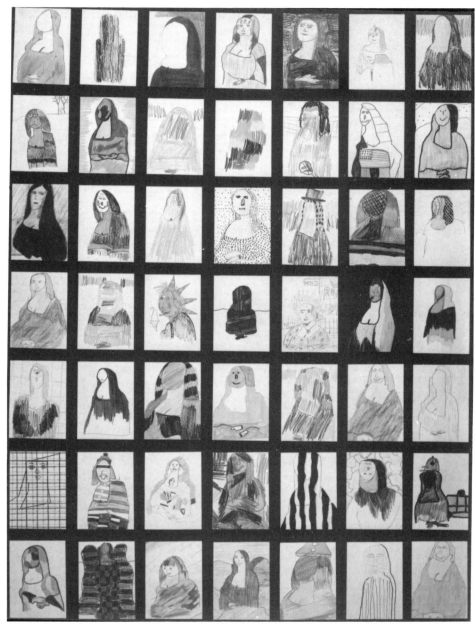

Fig. 6.5   49 variations on the Mona Lisa; various media (10 × 14cm).
12-year-olds, Audley Park School, Torquay. These variations on the
'Mona Lisa' were made following upon a discussion about the painting
and about the publication 'Mona Lisas' (Studio Vista), which contains the
work of many graphic designers who have responded playfully to this
archetypal image.

ism and fantasy), because they have begun to realize in their own response to images that images have meanings over and above their appearances.

It is natural for many children to want to draw their favourite paintings in support of their comments and written descriptions. For many, the drawing or copying of a painting is a genuine form of appraisal and may give them understanding of the work which would be difficult to achieve through the more formal means of language.

Direct Studies from Works of Art

There are various ways of working directly from works of art, whether in their original form or in reproduction. There has been considerable controversy surrounding the notion of copying or 'borrowing' from the work of other artists. Despite the fact that a great deal of copying is done in schools, the idea of using a painting or the reproduction of a painting in this kind of way has been seriously questioned by some teachers. There is a significant difference between an image created by an artist, in which he has observed and refashioned some aspect of the world, and the image created by the mechanical eye of the camera lens. By observing an artist's work, children can learn much about how things seen, imagined or remembered can be translated into media. Even in reproduction, it is difficult to observe any painting by Cézanne, Van Gogh or Matisse without being aware of the way in which the artist uses both pigment and colour. Once you move away from studio based work and into the environment, many of the phenomena we might want to ask children to observe and use are both complex and transitory – changes in light and in atmosphere and continuous movement make it very difficult for children to observe such things as water and clouds with any certainty. Children can learn much about how to paint clouds by observing paintings by Constable. Similarly, they can gain better understanding of the rendering of water through studying David Hockney's paintings of swimming pools.

Children in primary schools seem to be cheerfully uninhibited in their 'borrowing' from works of art. They enjoy the challenge of making a picture 'like' that painted by a famous artist and one which they themselves like (figures 6.6–6.8). In their first two years in secondary schools, they respond particularly well to paintings that are descriptive and which in reproduction provide helpful evidence of the way that paint has been used and applied, as in the work of many of the Impressionists and Post-Impressionists. As the need to make more complex images of personal meaning grows in children, they can gain much support through the study of work of painters, illustrators and graphic designers who have dealt with similar problems. There is some limited value in copying a favourite painting in its entirety – especially when the work is chosen to help the student deal with certain elements or properties in the making of the copy.

Working directly from works of art has a more immediate and general use when different methods are used to focus the children's attention upon particular things they can learn through the study of a painting. Perhaps the most familiar of these is the use of various kinds of viewfinders and grids to select one part of the work that provides interest and useful study. Many paintings can be used in this way as the vehicle for group work in colour: a reproduction is divided into sections and each child in the group has to reproduce that section carefully enough to match its neighbours. Similarly, a slide of a painting may be projected onto a wall that has been divided into a grid. The children choose one section for themselves that they like and want to match in other media. Asking children to translate a section of a painting, or a detail within it, into other media, reworking in paper or fabric collage for example, can usefully focus attention upon properties of colour, surface and design within the painting (figure 6.10).

Since children's experience of works of art is predominantly through reproduction, it is also worth using the fact that we become familiar with a work on a very different scale to the

Fig. 6.6. After 'Favourite courtyard at Fez' by Patrick Proctor; water-colour (30 × 21cm). 10-year-old, Woodford Junior School, Plympton.

Fig. 6.7 After 'Self portrait' by Vincent Van Gogh; powder colour (24 × 28cm). 11-year-old, Woodfield Junior School, Plymouth.

Direct studies from works of art. These copies or 'borrowings' were made by children from paintings they found particularly pleasing – either for their content or because of the way the artist has used colour. All of them show how much children are encouraged to use colour and paint very positively when they are asked to study a painting very carefully.

169

Fig. 6.8 Detail study from 'The doctor' by Sir Luke Fildes; charcoal and pastel (19 × 24cm). 11-year-old, Manor Junior School, Ivybridge.

Fig. 6.9 Detail study from 'Portrait of the Infanta' by Velasquez; tempera (22 × 35cm). 15-year-old, Uffculme School.

original. Where possible, it is useful to match a poster reproduction of a painting which may be close to the size of the original work with a set of postcards of the same painting, so that children can have their own small copy of the work being observed. Similar useful comparison can be made between a photographic reproduction of a painting and an enlarged projection of a slide of the same painting. Some good use has been made of group work combined with projection to enable a class of children to reproduce very large paintings at their original size. The sheer scale of some paintings needs to be experienced for them to be properly valued. In one school, all the first-year children combined to reproduce one of the passages from Stanley Spencer's war-time paintings of engineering shipyards on the Clyde. Interesting work results from the reverse process – accepting the scale of the postcard and slide and asking children to work from these sources on the same scale as the reproduction (figure 6.12).

Paintings can also be used to set the children more subtle problems. It is usefully demanding to ask children to rework a painting in a different colour range, especially when different groups within the class are asked to use different combinations of colours. This can lead to some useful discussion about the way in which colour change can affect the mood of a painting. Older children can be set the challenging task of taking one painting and reworking it in the style of another artist – this works particularly well when they have already been comparing paintings similar in content but from very different schools of painting.

Although works of art are useful reference material and can be used in the variety of ways described here, there is no doubt that their principal value lies within their use as a means to focus children's attention upon things seen or experienced.

Works of Art as Focus for Things Seen

Some paintings are simple to reconstruct within the art room. Van Gogh's 'Yellow chair with a

Fig. 6.10   Collage in paper and fabric based upon study of paintings by Gauguin; mixed media (36 × 50cm). 12-year-old, Plymstock.

pipe' and Matisse's 'Still life with a goldfish bowl', for example, may interestingly be compared with something very close to their real equivalent displayed alongside the painting. Discussion about and comparison between the real and painted images can be valuable starting points for the children's own painting of the same theme. You can use several paintings presented in association with the familiar clutter of still-life groups to provoke discussion about the different ways in which artists have responded to this kind of source material.

Fig. 6.11 Drawing using grids – after study of polaroid portraits by David Hockney; pencil (25 × 25cm). 13-year-old, Eggbuckland School, Plymouth.

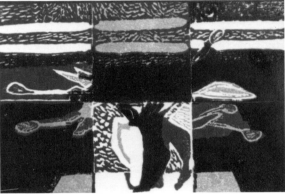

Fig. 6.12 Responding to the scale of works of art seen in reproduction; lino cuts based on postcard reproductions. 14-year-olds, Eggbuckland School, Plymouth.

Works of art may also be used to help children deal with the more complex problems of working in the environment. Example 3 describes how one teacher working with 8/9-year-olds on the theme of city-scapes used reference to the views from the window, photographs of other cities and the drawings of Paul Klee to support the children's looking. The Klee drawings were ideally matched to the level at which children of this age both observe and invent within their own drawings (figure 6.13).

In another school, a collection of original prints by different artists, all drawn from observation of different aspects of Dartmoor, were used as starting points and reference in association with the children's own visit to the moor and their own drawings and paintings of similar subject matter.

Evidence of the way that the artist works – to demonstrate the stages that take place between the first observations and the finished work – can also be used in support of children's work. David Hockney's working methods have been well documented, and a preliminary study of the way that he collects information and draws from the environment were used in one school to help children key into the ways that they might use the rather stark and formal landscape of the school. The children discussed and examined the subtle ways that Hockney gives significance to his drawings and paintings of buildings and fragments of buildings and used similar working methods in preparation for their own work (figure 6.14). In another school, similar working methods were used to help the children recreate the working method and atmosphere of another Hockney painting, 'Pool with two figures'.

There are many interesting examples of the way that works of art may be used to support children in their drawing and painting of figures and groups of figures within the environment. This is an area of work in which most children find difficulty once they need to move beyond

Using works of art as the focus for things seen and experienced. In these examples the children were asked to compare their view of familiar scenes or figures with the way these were represented in the work of various artists. The work of art became a focus for the children's perception and obviously both influenced and supported their own representations of these experiences.

Fig. 6.13   City-scapes based upon observation of drawings by Paul Klee and of views from the classroom window; Biro and felt pen (8 × 38cm). 9-year-olds, Whitleigh Junior School, Plymouth.

Fig. 6.14 Photographic study, drawing and painting of part of the school, following upon discussions about the working methods used by David Hockney in his paintings of built environments; 15-year-old, Estover School, Plymouth.

the drawing of a single posed figure. Example 3, 'Children's games', at the end of Chapter 5 has already described one such case. Example 4 in this chapter details one teacher's attempt to generate some feeling in the traditional life-drawing exercise as preparation for examination. The use of reference to and reconstruction of Henry Moore's wartime drawings of people sheltering and sleeping underground proved valuable towards helping the children to explore the form of the figure through its draping with some perception (figure 6.15). Similar use of lay figures and dolls, posed and lit to correspond to figures observed in paintings chosen for their dramatic content, did much to encourage a livelier approach by the children to the traditional figure composition.

In all this kind of work it is interesting to see

Fig. 6.15 Sleepers. Paintings of draped figures in the studio following upon observation of and discussion about the wartime underground shelter drawings by Henry Moore; powder colour (45 × 50cm). 14-year-old, Plymouth High School for Girls.

Fig. 6.16 Pop art variation and comment upon the painting 'Mr and Mrs Clark and Percy' by David Hockney; powder colour and inks. 15-year-old, Eggbuckland School, Plymouth.

175

the interaction of the children between what they have observed and their view of what has been achieved by another artist. The range and quality of response suggests that using works of art in these various ways helps to extend the children's understanding of what it is possible to achieve within a drawing or painting. They are challenged by the confrontation with a work of art – even when it is only postcard sized – and in this challenge engage with a greater vocabulary of possibilities.

The Use of Works of Art in Support of Children's Personal Development

The work of other artists can be used as source material for the children's own personal work. Paintings – through their content – can encourage children to be inventive, sometimes at the simple level of story-telling. David Hockney's 'Mr and Mrs Clark and Percy' is one of those paintings that lends itself admirably to different kinds of surmise, as does Gainsborough's 'Mr and Mrs Graham'. There is something about the formal family group that encourages children to ask questions: How did this painting come to be painted? What happened before and after? What kind of people are they really like when they are not posing for an artist? How would I represent my own family within this kind of convention – which room and which possessions would best illustrate or flatter the status of my parents?

Imagining the painting as one still frame within a film can lead to interesting conjecture about what happened five minutes before or after (figures 6.17 and 6.18)!

The work of other artists may also be used to help children see how they can make image-making say things that have personal meaning and significance over and above appearance. Older children are frequently required to work on themes which make demands upon their abilities to use images in this kind of way. When faced with the problem of responding to such themes as 'Familiar and unfamiliar', 'Distortion' or 'Metamorphosis', it is of considerable help to children if

they are given access to reproductions of the work of other artists who have explored similar areas of concern.

Sometimes it is possible to make an inventive match between the work of one school of artists and a visual problem of concern to children. One teacher used medieval ikons with his students as the basis for exploring the theme of figures under stress (figure 6.19). The same teacher also used the Elizabethan miniature as a starting point for the children's paintings of contemporary heroes (figure 6.20).

It is clear that children do benefit considerably from the opportunity to examine their own personal and expressive work against that which has been achieved by other artists. This has some value where the children can be given access to the work of other artists in reproduction. It takes on an altogether deeper significance when children can be given experience of original works or direct contact with a contemporary artist at work through the 'Artists in schools' programme.

Artists and Galleries

Children's access to original works of art is very dependent upon local circumstances. About one third of the local education authorities have collections of original works of art that are available for loan to schools. These range from those as impressive as the Leicestershire collection, which includes major works by leading contemporary painters and sculptors, to modest collections of prints and drawings mainly by local artists.

Access to galleries is equally varied. If you teach in London or in one of the major provincial cities, you are able to give your children generous experience of good collections of work and, in many cases, you will have the back-up and support of education officers and working spaces within the galleries. It is an enormous advantage to have a good permanent collection of work which you can get to know well and which you can use selectively within reasonable travelling

Fig. 6.17 Reproduction of painting 'General and Mrs Francis Dundee' by Raeburn.

Fig. 6.18 'General and Mrs Dundee – five minutes later'; tempera (36 × 50cm). 16-year-old, Ilfracombe School.

EXAMPLE 2

a parallel group who were asked to make a painting based on the written appraisal they had been given.

Pupils in the first group were specifically asked to produce a piece of imaginative writing, rather than just a straightforward description. The symmetry in the picture was most often interpreted in terms of life and death, or good and evil ('one side is alive and bright, the other is more abstract . . . the two sides seem to symbolize either life or death'). Some elements of the picture were almost universally misinterpreted, most commonly the repeated image of the hand and egg in the background which became 'some sort of animal in the hills', or 'a grey figure', even 'a Yeti', and for some reason these were emphasized when the descriptions were translated back into visual terms.

Unlike the first exercise, where children were working in isolation on their own individual pictures, here the pupils in both groups (writers and painters) were working from a common starting point, and a concensus of opinion was quickly reached between children sitting close together. So the chess board became an important element in one group of compositions, while in others it was only a minor detail.

As the paintings were nearing completion, pupils in the second group were allowed to see the original reproduction, and this helped them to resolve some of the details in their own pictures (amid accusations that the first group hadn't given them enough information, particularly in regard to the relative scale of the objects described).

Despite the obvious difficulties in interpreting the content of Dali's picture, the original painting received widespread approval.

3 Children were allowed to choose a reproduction of a particular painting that they liked. They were then asked to produce a new piece of work based on this painting, working directly from the reproduction.

Pupils' interest was aroused by the individual pictures used in the first exercise, and they asked if they could work directly from the reproductions (often the one that they had studied and had made a written description of). After careful study and preparatory drawings, they were asked to make a new version of the painting by rearranging the composition, or by selecting just a part of the composition (perhaps by the use of a viewfinder), or isolating one figure from a group of figures, at all times trying to retain accuracy of representation of the original.

Their main problem was in trying to reproduce an oil painting technique in a water-based medium, particularly when working from portraits. Some pupils' work was very imaginative, but in general the most successful were those which deviated very little from the original.

(All three of these projects were carried out with third- and fourth-year pupils, 13/15 years-old, in groups of 25 and of mixed ability, within a secondary modern school.)

List of reproductions used in the first exercise

The Tempest *(Giorgione)*
The Land of Cockayne *(Bruegel)*
The Card Players *(Cézanne)*
The Triumph of Death *(Bruegel)*
The Peaceable Kingdom *(Hicks)*
The Conversion of Saul *(Bruegel)*
The Starry Night *(Van Gogh)*
Luncheon In The Studio *(Manet)*
The Beggars *(Bruegel)*
The Parable of the Blind *(Bruegel)*
The Arnolfini Wedding *(Van Eyck)*
Christina's World *(Wyeth)*
The Duel (Mephistopheles I) *(Munch)*
Nighthawks *(Hopper)*
The Village Street *(Munch)*
House by a Railroad *(Hopper)*
The Peasant Wedding *(Bruegel)*
The Bellini Family *(Degas)*
Angry Masks *(Ensor)*
The Collector *(Daumier)*
The Therapeutist *(Magritte)*
The Lacemaker *(Vermeer)*
Gertrude Stein *(Picasso)*
Interior at Antibes *(Bonnard)*
The Painter And His Model *(Matisse)*
The Temptation of St Anthony *(Bosch)*
The Saltimbanques *(Picasso)*

Island of the Dead *(Bocklin)*
The Balcony *(Manet)*
Into The World Came A Soul Named Ida *(Albright)*
The Vision after the Sermon *(Gauguin)*
Arrangement in Grey and Black No. 1 *(Whistler)*
The Ship of Fools *(Bosch)*
The Fall of Icarus *(Bruegel)*
Ia Orana Maria *(Gauguin)*
Sunday Afternoon on the Grande Jatte *(Seurat)*
The Anguish of Departure *(de Chirico)*
The Lonely Ones (Two People) *(Munch)*
The Passion of Sacco and Vanzetti *(Shahn)*
Bonjour Monsieur Gauguin *(Gauguin)*
Mystery and Melancholy of a Street *(de Chirico)*
Executions of the 3rd of May *(Goya)*
Hotel by a Railroad *(Hopper)*
Evening (The Yellow Boat) *(Munch)*
The Poor Fisherman *(Puvis de Chavannes)*
The Dream *(Rousseau)*
Apparition of Face and Fruit-dish *(Dali)*
Uncle And Niece *(Degas)*
The Sleeping Gypsy *(Rousseau)*
Portrait of Emile Zola *(Manet)*

Rob Chapman   April 1984

EXAMPLE 3

child-like style being one they could identify with and understand. They saw a man recording his immediate environment in the same way as we ask them to do on many occasions.

Children do need to be reassured that art is relevant to them and that it has its own value to both people in its own day and to us now. This became clear when this same group of children visited the 'Alive to it all' exhibition at Plymouth's City Art Gallery and Museum, which included sketches by Paul Klee that were of a very naive nature. Here the children were most unimpressed and indeed let down. They felt that he (and they) could have done better.

Since this work, even a year later, the children constantly make references to these sources, saying with confidence that people and pictures are 'like Klee' or 'like Lowry'. They have continued to build on these references, and others like them, in the development of their own visual libraries.

Alison Brachtvogel
Whitleigh Junior School

EXAMPLE 4

Solving problems (see pages 174–6)

Kate Watkins   *Head of Art Department, Notre Dame RC Girls'*
School, Plymouth

Introduction

I see critical studies in art history as a way of opening up to children new aspects of their culture and environment. I want them to be able to form personal judgements, and have the vocabulary to express these judgements, both in relation to their own work and that of artists past and present.

I am more concerned with using artists' work to help my pupils gain awareness of design, composition, colour, social behaviour, technique, than being concerned about the historical dates and facts. I want the child to be concerned emotionally with what the artist was trying to say, and how we relate to these emotions today. The images presented should relate to the period they were produced in and be understood in relation to other aspects of learning.

I mostly use critical studies in art history to solve problems in practical work. As an example, I quote my fourth-years' work because of the problem they met in dealing with light falling on forms, particularly the human form. The girls, when drawing each other, often became so involved with details of figure and clothes, that the 'mass' of the body shapes became lost through ineffective use and interpretation of light.

My answer on this occasion was to talk about the drawings made by sculptors, and how a sculptor sees in a different way to a painter. I used Henry Moore as an example, and cited his drawings made during the war of people sleeping and resting in the underground shelters. I showed the group – 24 girls – examples of his drawings, and discussed with them how the drawings differed from those of a painter. We looked at the marks he made to describe form, and the lines and the media he used to create the final effect of the drawings.

I asked two girls to wrap themselves in blankets and lie close together on a central raised platform. Taking drawing materials that were mobile and easy to use, e.g. charcoal, chalks, pastels, coloured pens and crayons, I asked the girls to concentrate on the forms they could see. They were to try and interpret them in a similar style to the drawings we had been discussing. I wanted clear definition of light on the

189

EXAMPLE 4

forms; they must try and hold a mental picture of the shape of the body covered by the blanket. The Henry Moore book was passed around the group for closer inspection during the lesson, so each girl saw his work in detail but, in fact, visually it did not overpower or heavily influence the work being done. The previous discussion had the greater effect. The girls were searching with more confidence for form, and using light to describe it. Their technique was influenced by Henry Moore's style, but was not a direct copy.

After four different drawings, we discussed the results which were, on the whole, exciting and very different from any previous work. They had to take one drawing and develop it in any way they chose. Some saw landscapes, others needed to retain reality and placed their figures within a setting. It proved to be a valuable set of drawings, and the knowledge gained has been used and seen again in some later studies.

Another example of critical studies being used was in the context of first-year work. The first-years were looking at 'themselves' as part of a project. We had a group of them sitting together, some carrying open umbrellas, for the form to draw. They produced two drawings in the space of a double lesson, and moved around to draw from different views as well as to see each other's work. In the next lesson, we talked about where one might see a group of people sitting and standing in a similar way. We decided one did not often see people today relaxing in the same way, unless they were watching a sport, or in the park or on the beach.

I produced a collection of reproductions showing how artists have drawn and painted people relaxing or sitting in groups. We decided many looked posed and unreal, especially by today's standards. They liked some Dutch Genre paintings and French Impressionist artists who seemed to capture real people doing everyday things. We chose one artist, Seurat, and studied his pictures, particularly the painting 'La Grande Jatte', and the style he used to put the paint onto the canvas. They particularly liked the colour and light effect he produced in his paintings.

Working in groups of two or three, and using their own drawings for reference, they tried to produce a picture of people relaxing in today's world. The umbrellas could be part of the picture, for sun or rain, or other ideas drawn in to replace them. They tried to copy the style of painting used by Seurat or any other of the artists they admired. One important part of the painting was the scale. They worked on

A1 sheets of paper to make it possible for them to work together on the same picture.

Through study of the painters' style and composition, the girls learned a lot about the artists' work, as well as thinking more deeply about what they were doing. Socially, they were able to discuss with each other or as a group how people relax today compared with 100 years ago, or more. Dress was seen as important: people 'then' dressed up to be seen relaxing, and yet it looked difficult to relax in those sorts of clothes. In contrast, today, we appear more casually dressed, or even 'undressed', when relaxing. Social behaviour – the accepted behaviour of the day – reflected on how people dressed, where they were seen, and how they displayed themselves in public. Artists became reporters.

This project led to much discussion between pupils and thought about how much we see around us reflecting the social behaviour accepted by our society. The paintings studied were no longer pretty pictures to hang on museum walls or to be found in books. They became like a newspaper reporting on life, events and feelings of the day.

I consider it a very valuable and useful way to study and help children overcome practical problems they face by studying the way artists tackle the same problems. The study of artists' work, techniques and styles becomes a real thing and not removed into history and the world of books and facts to learn. Art, our heritage of the past and present, can be seen as a relevant way to report and question society. Art is 'real' and for today. It is not something that has a mystique about it that only 'clever' people can understand.

One of the duties of an art teacher is to help children become confident enough to understand and express valid opinions about their past and present environment. 'Art' must be seen as part of the record of life to be enjoyed by the majority, and not a culture for the few.

I found that the most successful work with which the children became involved was when we were problem solving, and not setting up artificial problems. In the two examples I have discussed, the fourth-year work was based on this concept. The first-year pupils' work showed how one can discover information about society from works of art, and make history an intensely living thing. Hopefully, it will cause enquiry into, and comparison between, the symbols of modern life, and its values to be questioned.

Kate Watkins ATD

EXAMPLE 5

EXAMPLE 5

Gallery study sheets

Robert Hooper   *Head of Art Department, Tavistock School*

Used in conjunction with the following exhibition:

'The artist as photographer', Royal Albert Memorial Museum and Art Gallery, Exeter, 1983.

PAINTER AS PHOTOGRAPHER   WORKSHEET NO: 1

NAME ....

SCHOOL ....

TEACHER ....

1. Go and look at the photograph illustrated above. Write the name of the
    artist and the title in the box:

2. Look at the photograph carefully. Which of the following statements about
    the photograph is most correct? Underline it.

    The artist took the picture because he:

        (a) thought it looked like an animal
        (b) was studying dead trees
        (c) liked the effect of light and shade
        (d) was interested in line and rhythm
        (e) thought it symbolised strength
        (f) was reminded of winter
        (g) .... (your idea)

3. Now find other photographs in the exhibition, and write their titles and
    the names of the artists in the box, that are mostly about:

    (a) Slight differences in colour

    (b) Reflections

    (c) Distance

    (d) Pattern

    (e) Movement

193

EXAMPLE 5

PAINTER AS PHOTOGRAPHER   WORKSHEET NO: 2

NAME ....

SCHOOL ....

TEACHER ....

1. Find the photograph in the exhibition that you think the illustration
   is based on. Name the artist and the title.

2. The Artist took many photographs to help him in his work, designing
   posters. He was not afraid to change things to make them more decorative.
   Compare the illustration, based on one of his posters, with the photograph.
   One of the most obvious changes is the different background. Can you see
   three other main changes? Describe them.

   (a)

   (b)

   (c)

3. Find a photograph in the exhibition that would be a good starting point
   for a poster. On a separate piece of paper, make a drawing from it.
   Change anything that you want, either to make it more decorative or to
   improve it in some other way. Write your name and school clearly on the
   top before you start.

   Write the name of the artist and title of the photograph here.

   Write the main changes you have made here. Carry on overleaf if you
   run out of room.

PAINTER AS PHOTOGRAPHER   WORKSHEET NO: 3 PORTRAITS

NAME ....

SCHOOL ....

TEACHER ....

1. Find the photograph in the exhibition illustrated above. Egon Schiele
    contorted his face while it was taken. There are many portraits and
    self portraits in the exhibition. The above is an example of one that
    is funny and at the same time strange.

    Can you find examples in the exhibition that show people as:

    _____
    (a) Lonely ....

    _____
    (b) Tired ....

    _____
    (c) Stupid ....

    _____
    (d) Dignified ....

    _____
    (e) Moving ....

    _____
    (f) Strong ....

    _____
    (g) Having fun ....

    _____
    (h) Beautiful or handsome ....

    _____
    (i) Thoughtful ....

    _____
    (j) Frightened ....

    _____
    (k) Relaxed ....
    _____

    Try to find a different example for each. Write the name of the artist
    and the title in the spaces.

    On a separate piece of paper make a drawing from the photograph you think
    works best from your list above. Try to bring out the quality you think
    is shown.

    Write your name and school clearly on your paper.

EXAMPLE 6

EXAMPLE 6

An artist in school

Helen Stokes *Deputy Head Teacher, Glen Park Primary School, Plympton*

ex-Teacher in charge of art, Thornbury Primary School, Plymouth

Report on the visit of 'artist in residence', Grace Erikson, weaver, Thornbury Primary School, from 20/6/83 to 1/7/83. Age group: 10/11-year-olds.

Grace's brief was to continue with her own weaving so that the children could observe how she worked, to talk to the children as a group about her life and work as a weaver and to advise any children who might seek her advice during the course of the two weeks.

Using Grace's weavings as a starting point, seven members of staff were asked to develop language, weaving, drawing, creative needlework, pottery and drama. A 'granny', who enjoyed weaving as a hobby, proved to be an invaluable member of the team.

It was decided that language work should follow on from a close observation of Grace's weavings, or drama, art and craft activities. The children were allowed as much time as they needed to complete each area of work, and their progress was monitored by the staff at the end of each day. Initially, the children were divided into mixed ability groups and, despite the flexibility of the programme, the balance of numbers in each group was not significantly changed.

Having viewed Grace's work earlier in the term, the staff decided that the 'umbrella' title, 'Inside, outside', was a suitable theme for the two weeks; a number of her works showed the interior and exterior of houses, a number were the expression of her thoughts, the very process of weaving could be seen as moving in and out with the threads. This abstract title offered a wide area for exploration beyond the specific subjects of Grace's weavings but retained the link.

We were privileged because Grace chose to start a new weaving, at the start of the two weeks, based on her present home and her immediate surroundings. She suspended her loom from a beam in one of the classrooms and displayed her range of wools on the classroom shelves. She suspended a mini loom from a nearby beam so that children could take it in turns to work on a hanging loom, working in a situation akin to her own; the subject was their own choice.

As the first hour of the day was devoted to the teaching of maths, the programme occupied 3½ hours daily for two weeks. On the Friday preceding 20th June, Grace came into school and mounted a number of the weavings in two class bases (we are an open-plan school) and in the dining hall. She also set up her own loom. The children were extremely interested in the setting-up process and were overawed by the size of the weavings.

Starting point

On the first morning of her two weeks' stay, Grace gave a short talk and answered the children's questions. The questions reflected their previous experience of weaving and were about technique and inspiration, finance, time, source of materials, and Grace's own background. We discussed in detail the themes of the hangings that were immediately visible. During the second week, Grace again talked to the children about her work, this time using slides.

Weaving

The children were encouraged to observe closely Grace's technique, her choice of colour, the textures of her wools and her artistic interpretation: throughout the two weeks, she gave them advice. After making initial sketches, the children wove individual pieces on small looms. They used wools of different colours and thicknesses. The wools had been stranded and hung in colour batches on the wall; this made selection easier and encouraged greater discrimination. The first group worked all day for a full week on the weavings. Not all were completed, but the standard achieved was high. Most of the children worked on abstract compositions of shape and colour rather than specific objects.

At the start of the second week, a different group began. The looms were warped ready and this resulted in a speedier start and completion of the weavings. This third-year group also concentrated on technique. Some of the group were introduced to the art of rag-rug making because Grace had brought a plaited and coiled rug in with her; they found the coiling difficult – hooking might be a satisfying alternative. They used magnifying glasses and viewers to do close-up pastel drawings of their own weavings.

EXAMPLE 6

Over the two weeks, children took it in turns to work on the mini suspended loom that Grace had set up near her own. Artistically, the result was not particularly inspiring, but the children were engrossed as they worked. They obviously found it satisfying and had no problem picking up where another person had left off.

Drawing
Initially, children examined a chosen weaving closely and then, using focusing devices or magnifying glasses, chose a small area to reproduce on a larger scale. Pastels were used for this work. Two children chose to examine the patterns made by houses in one of Grace's weavings and subsequently worked on making patterns with houses of their own creation, using black fibre-tip pens. A variety of illustrations from children's books were used to provide ideas for drawing simple houses.

A group of children drew a classroom chair in pencil and later chose one of the stylized chairs in Grace's weavings to reproduce. Lots of interesting discussions arose as to why Grace had chosen such a simple form.

Later on, the artwork was linked more specifically with language or drama as well as with the actual weavings. For instance, children working on poems about houses then focused on the 'Four rooms' weaving and made small paper 3D room interiors that contained a favourite piece of furniture. Other children, who had been reading poetry or literature about gardens, created an imaginary dream-like garden in 3D using card and felt-tip pen.

Children who had been reading poems about caged animals (continuing the 'Inside, outside' theme) worked in charcoal and chalk to draw a favourite toy animal, brought into school, in a cage.

A great deal of Grace's work dealt with thoughts, dreams, wishes, fears etc., and we took this opportunity to get the children to explore their own thoughts. They worked on careful self portraits in pencil, using mirrors, and then drew small pictures in the region of the brain to illustrate their different thoughts. They also wrote down the meaning of each picture. Some children chose to write first and then draw. The children were involved in an amazing amount of discussion throughout this exercise.

They were fascinated by Grace's tools and were encouraged to look at them closely and draw them. A few drew the weaving looms in great detail and, throughout, questioned Grace as to the purpose of the components. These children then wrote an analytical account of how a loom functions.

Throughout all the artwork, language became very important and relevant to their discussions; words such as texture, colour, pattern, shape, design, space, design, simplicity etc. The children had to analyse how the weaving was carried out, how long the work took, why certain shades of tone were used. They were asked to interpret certain features of Grace's hangings. For example, we asked one child to guess and then to ask his friends why there were red lines running across the trees; this aroused curiosity and the responses reflected careful thought. Grace did not offer her own explanation until the end of the two weeks.

Pottery   Two groups were able to participate in pottery over the period of the two weeks.

Group 1
Theme: 'This should have been my house.'
The children's attention was directed to three aspects of Grace's weavings:
1 symbolic representation;
2 the changing of reality to suit Grace's own desires and imagination;
3 the interiors and exteriors of houses.

Form of work: three slab tiles
1 My garden
2 My house – exterior
3 Inside my room

The tiles were in high relief and were joined together (after firing) with a coarse thread.

Group 2
Theme: 'Boxes.'
This work was inspired by Grace's use of boxes, box house shapes, tumbling boxes, the theme of 'Inside, outside'. The children discussed and considered the relationship between the outside of a box and its inside, the expected contents of a box compared with contents you might not expect.

Form of work: from slab tiles, the children built a diagonal section of a cube that showed the exterior and the interior.

7 THE PLACE OF THE CRAFTS

Differentiation between Craft and Design Subjects

This chapter is not about how to teach the crafts. There is a wealth of published material on every aspect of making and designing in the different craft areas. I am more concerned here to examine the place of the crafts in schools, which is complicated by the fact that the crafts are taught under three different subject headings: art and design, CDT (craft design and technology) and home economics. Of all the crafts, only print-making and ceramics are almost exclusively taught by art teachers in art departments.

In the past twenty years, there has been a steady growth in the emergence and establishment of design courses and design faculties in schools, and the different concerns and interests of teachers of art, CDT and home economics have been focused and brought together in an attempt to find some common ground — especially in their teaching of craft and design. Even where these subjects are grouped together to form a design faculty, it is comparatively rare to find within that group of teachers a consistent attitude towards the teaching of the crafts.

In many design departments there has been too much emphasis upon trying to relate the crafts to some generalized notion of design, to which the constituent subjects must conform, rather than on seeking for ways to rationalize and balance the different kinds of learning which the teaching of craft can promote.

The inappropriateness of the current tendency to classify the crafts by their materials rather than by the resulting experience can be seen when we consider, for example, that you can teach ceramics as a collection of necessary skills to make such things as thumb pots, coil pots, slabbed ware, pressed mould dishes etc., or you can teach ceramics as an extension of drawing, encouraging the children to use clay as a flexible and expressive medium in which to make three-dimensional images of things seen or that have personal meaning to them. Work in clay can explore such formal qualities as surface, form, pattern and structure where the emphasis may be upon making equivalents for natural and man-made forms both observed and analysed. Ceramics can also be taught as problem solving: designing and making clay forms to satisfy given functions or requirements. A similar variety of experience can be described for work in any of the familiar materials we use in the teaching of crafts in our schools.

If you are working with teachers of other subjects to plan a programme of work in art, craft and design, it will be more productive to look at the different kinds of learning you want to promote across the material areas, rather than basing your programme on giving equal access to a range of materials. The three dominant processes taught through the crafts are:

visual enquiry, where the work in craft grows out of an exploration of the visual world, either objectively through observation of things seen and translated into media, or analytically through an exploration of materials of the visual elements that contribute to our perception of the world, e.g. colour, structure, surface, pattern etc;

acquisition of skills, where craft making can only follow upon the students being taught a number of basic skills and processes, which once learnt can be applied to the making of certain things;

problem solving, where the work in craft is determined by problems set or defined. These can range from experimenting with materials to explore general principles, to work where clear-cut problems are presented to the children, which can be solved through designing and making an artefact.

Obviously enough, none of these processes are exclusive, and in a successful craft programme all should be present at some stage or other. Where a programme of craft teaching is being shared by teachers of different subjects, it is paramount that they should keep under review both the content of their work and the processes they are teaching through their craft, in order to ensure that the best possible use is made of that time set aside for the crafts.

Careful monitoring is even more important in the many schools where the crafts are timetabled and taught through rotational systems, and where during the first two years of secondary schooling the children may move at half-termly intervals from one material to another. It is all too easy for there to be unnecessary repetition of concept and process as the children pass from clay to metal to wood to fabric etc!

It may make more sense for you and your colleagues to identify and balance your different approaches to the teaching of craft, rather than to pursue that common ground that is implied within the design education movement, where all too often what is achieved is the lowest common denominator of design rather than factors of quality.

The Relationship between Two-dimensional and Three-dimensional Work

In many art, craft and design departments or faculties, there have been serious attempts to try to find a pattern of working whereby the work of designing and making is supported by a programme of two-dimensional work in which children explore concepts or elements that feed

into the making activity. The notion of a basic design course was pioneered at the Bauhaus School in Germany in the 1930s and has had a significant influence upon work in the English art schools through the work of such teachers as Maurice de Sausmarez, Harry Thubron, Victor Passmore, Kurt Rowlands *et al.* In theory, and at a high level of practice, the system can work well as there are clearly a number of visual concepts that are common to many aspects of craft and design and which once understood can be applied to making in different materials.

In practice, in schools and with 11/12-year-olds, the basic design system has many drawbacks, the principal one being that it separates designing from making. In some schools, it has been assumed that 'basic design' (the study of colour, tone, surface, pattern, structure etc.) can be taught in much the same way as basic manual skills, rather like the traditional teacher of woodwork who insists on teaching his pupils all the basic operations of working in wood before they are allowed to make real things in wood!

There is no doubt that children can apply such basic visual skills as are taught through basic design systems, but only if the acquisition of the visual skill is immediately related to a real task. There is nothing more depressing than to put children through an intensive six-week programme in colour theory, only then to discover that they can't apply the theory to making a painting! The abstract nature of much basic design teaching, and the assumption that 11/12-year-olds can make that intellectual jump from theory to practice, can all too often only lead to rather low level pattern making in materials.

What is common to all crafts and to all crafts-people is not a collection of rather low level visual skills; it is more likely to be a common concern for the way that craft-making grows out of the following kind of process:

through drawing, an examination of the visual information offered by the natural and man-made world;

through analysis and selection, a focus on those

aspects of the world that motivate and inspire the individual craftsperson;

through exploration and manipulation of materials, an understanding of how they may be used to support the making of artefacts that have both quality and personal meaning.

If you have to share your teaching of craft with other subject teachers, and wish to seek some common ground for your teaching of the crafts, it may be more profitable to discuss and explore with them those common elements of observing, analysing, information collecting and material manipulation that are present in good craftsmanship, rather than the elementary visual skills that the children might need to acquire before they are allowed to make things.

Day-to-day Work in Schools

The day-to-day practice of the teaching of craft will be determined by the pattern of timetabling and subject organization adopted within your own school. There is considerable variety in practice. In some schools, art, CDT and home economics are autonomous departments. In others, they may be grouped to form a faculty with such various labels as 'art and design', 'design', 'creative design' etc. In some schools, you will find art as part of an even larger grouping within a 'creative arts faculty' which will also include music and drama and sometimes even physical education! Some schools choose to separate art from CDT and home economics and to form separate faculties of 'expressive arts' and 'craft and design'.

Within your own art department, there should be little difficulty in establishing a proper relationship between the more general work in drawing and painting and that in the crafts. There is a strong link between drawing and many of the crafts – notably in batik and print-making, and in ceramics when clay is used as a three-dimensional drawing medium.

There are logical links between the different crafts, as are demonstrated in Example 1, where

process in one craft can be linked directly to process in another as in the obvious link between slip trailing on clay and drawing with a tjanting in batik.

The original drawing or exploration will frequently need to be followed up by a further analysis through the use of materials, so that the children can begin to key into the particular disciplines of different materials and processes. Figures 7.1–7.3 illustrate the transition from making a drawing of a decayed tooth to simplifying the forms through paper collage in preparation for making a screen print.

Within the timetabling of art within your school, it should be possible to allocate at least one third of the time to work in one of the crafts during the first three years of secondary schooling. It is better to concentrate the work in craft to a limited number of materials and to look for an interesting balance rather than great variety. In one year, the balance may be between plastic materials and resistant materials – in another between using craft processes expressively or in a very disciplined way. It is certainly better to give sufficient time to one or two crafts, in order that good craft skills can be developed, rather than to attempt too many at too superficial a level.

As children grow in their skills and confidence in handling a particular craft, they need opportunities for greater specialism, and most art departments ought to be able to offer at least one craft course to those students opting to take art to examination level at 16-plus.

The overall success of the craft programme that is taught by teachers of different subjects will depend upon whether you and your colleagues have moved beyond a simple classification of the crafts by their material labels (woodwork, textiles, pottery, metalwork etc.) towards some serious discussion about the different experiences your crafts offer.

Many faculties have foundered where they have been established for the wrong reasons – as an administrative convenience, because the studios and workshops are physically related in a

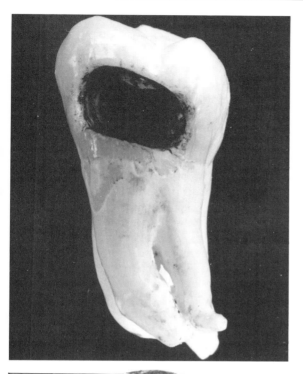

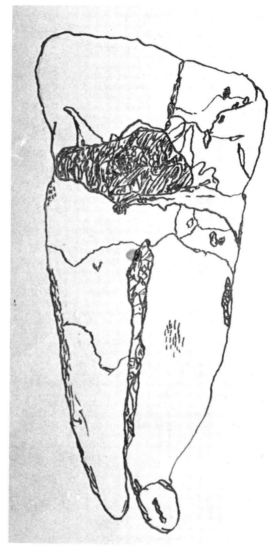

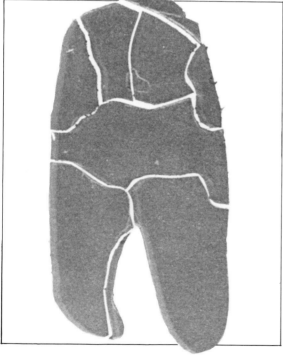

Working from observation through drawing and further analysis towards designing for a craft process. 15-year-old, Great Torrington School.

Fig. 7.1 (top left)   Photograph, decayed tooth.

Fig. 7.2 (right)   Drawing from decayed tooth.

Fig. 7.3 (bottom left)   Cut paper studies of decayed tooth made in preparation for a silk-screen print.

new building, because these subjects are seen as being 'practical', because it is assumed that they are all 'creative' in the same generalized way. Similarly, in theory, the block timetabling of the 'practical' subjects together should lead towards a better management of the teaching of craft. It is comparatively rare to find those subjects concerned using that flexibility that block time-tabling allows: establishing lead sessions and team teaching, alternating or changing the subject emphasis as a programme or theme develops, linking areas of work, alternating groups between teachers as new skills and concepts need to be fed into a project etc.

In some schools there is a conscious attempt to set up a sequence from one art or craft area to another, which makes for some kind of logic in that skills and concepts acquired with one teacher are used and built upon by the next teacher the child works with as, for example, when the art module in which the children explore colour and surface qualities is followed by a module in textiles where some of those principles may be applied. Although this is possible in the transfer from one workshop/studio to another, it is difficult to design a logical programme of this kind of linking right through the year, simply because not all the craft areas relate so directly to each other as in the example given.

Example 2 illustrates a good use of the carousel system and shows how in one design department there have been attempts to make links between the different crafts.

In other schools, there have been attempts to link the crafts thematically — so that in any one term or half-termly module, the children in different craft areas may be working on similar themes, which may include both a common lead session for all the children and some sharing of their work and experiences at the end of the module. Although there are some themes which can work well, and which are equally relevant to all the craft areas involved, they are limited in number and it is difficult to sustain a consistent programme throughout all the crafts that will work in this way and will not, at some stage, trivialize the work in some areas. Without careful planning, this method of working together within the crafts can lead to considerable repetition of both content and concepts.

The most successful plan seems to be where the teachers concerned have been able to agree upon a sequence of themes that are demanding yet general enough for each craft area to use on its own terms. In one school, the children in the first year move from the study of surface appearance to structure to movement in a variety of materials. The structured use of visual source material, worksheets and some lead sessions and team teaching help to make this progression understandable to the children, helped by the deliberate use of sharing and critical sessions at the end of each 'theme'. (See Example 3.)

In another school, the assumption that all the craft areas can share the same concerns is properly challenged and, within the time allocated to this variety of subjects, two modules a week are set aside for shared or combined work. Teachers of the different subjects concerned can choose to opt into this shared time or remain out of it. This has the advantage of bringing together for the shared work those teachers who have some understanding of and commitment to the principle and allowing those who are doubtful recruits to continue more confidently with their separate and more specialist concerns.

Whichever system you and your colleagues in other departments adopt, and with what degree of success, will depend upon how well you can jointly resolve the conflict between the need for children to have both a general understanding of the principles of designing and making and also enough time to develop sufficient skills and confidence to craft with some authority.

Fig. 7.4 Drawing three-dimensionally with clay, beach picnic. 11-year-old, Heavitree Middle School, Exeter.

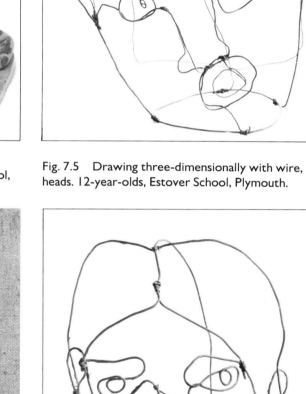

Fig. 7.5 Drawing three-dimensionally with wire, heads. 12-year-olds, Estover School, Plymouth.

Fig. 7.6 Trees; ceramic. 10-year-olds, Thornbury Primary School, Plymouth.

Using materials inventively to create images that are both determined and stimulated by the nature of the materials used. Good examples of image-making with materials associated with more conventional kinds of response.

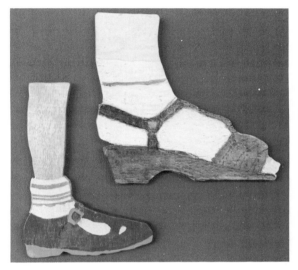

Fig. 7.7   Our leader; fabric collage. 14-year-old, Estover School, Plymouth.

Fig. 7.8   Our shoes; plywood and dyes. 12-year-olds, Wilcombe Middle School, Tiverton.

Fig. 7.9   Plate of cakes. 14-year-old, Clyst Vale College.

Reconstruction of familiar things in clay. These examples demonstrate the versatility of clay as a means to analyse and record the appearance of familiar things. The process of translation into clay requires children to consider the formal qualities within the things they are describing and to become very involved with analysing the structure of these forms.

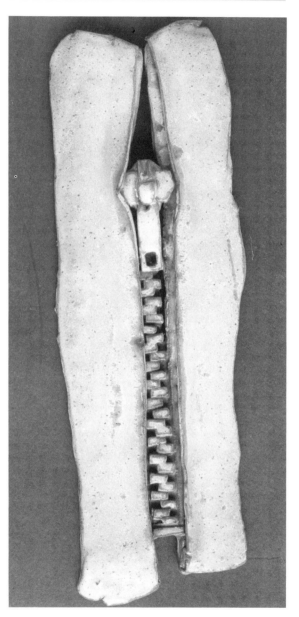

Fig. 7.10 Hand bag. 13-year-old, Estover School, Plymouth.

Fig. 7.11 Zip. 13-year-old, Estover School, Plymouth

Problem solving with materials.

Fig. 7.12 Plywood landscape. 12-year-old, Wilcombe Middle School, Tiverton.

Fig. 7.13 Jigsaw puzzles. 13-year-olds, Wilcombe Middle School, Tiverton.

Fig. 7.14 Figure.

The expressive use of clay. A figure based upon observation of the characteristic expressions of members of staff and children within this school.

EXAMPLE 1

Print-making connections

Neil White   *Art Adviser for Hillingdon*

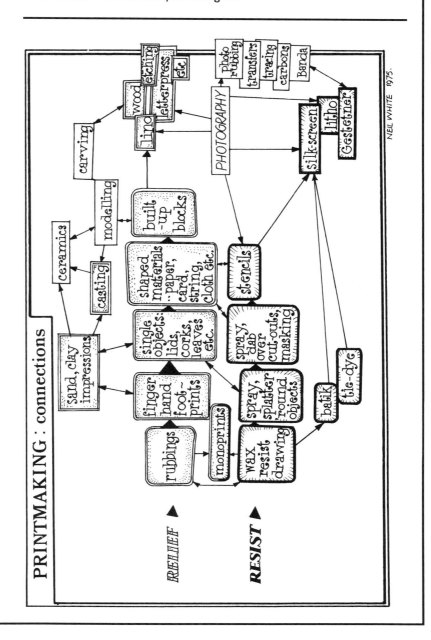

209

EXAMPLE 2

EXAMPLE 2

First-year course in art and design, King Edward VIth School, Totnes (see page 204)

Colin Bigwood   *Head of Art Department*

During the first two years, the children are able to work in all the basic material areas which the Art, Home Economics and Technical Studies Departments can offer.

The main aims are to achieve some understanding of the relationship of various art/craft activities, together with a quite comprehensive grounding in material/tool techniques, basic visual concepts and 'language'. It is a *foundation* course. Advantage is gained by year block timetabling, co-operation and resources of the three departments and smaller group working.

The outline syllabus suggests a number of basic visual concepts that should be covered during the first two years. It is hoped that these will be covered through two means:

through exploration of material/tool operations;

through study of natural and man-made environments and objects, together with the emotional and imaginative/inventive responses to organized situations.

The two means constantly overlap. Likewise, the exploration of different concepts will overlap depending upon the context within which the exploration is placed, e.g. a child making a ceramic tile based on a study of natural surfaces will be exploring:

(a) the effect of different materials upon the surface – clay;
(b) repetition of unit marks to create a surface pattern;
(c) use of light/shadow to create tonal surface variety;
(d) tactile properties of surface;
(e) effect of changing scale in translating source material into a particular medium.

This may appear difficult and beyond young students' understanding, but such concepts can be discussed and demonstrated by a sympathetic and experienced teacher using suitable language and examples from the environment.

Outline syllabus The syllabus does not specify in depth the content in which the material/visual experience should be studied as this will vary from teacher to teacher, depending upon their particular strengths and interests. A general plan is laid down so that a particular sequence is followed which will enable staff in the team to understand the overall pattern and perhaps allow some linking from one material area to another. The course is changing as improvements and experiments take place. Staff meetings are held to unify or modify detail through experience, although frequent small 'design' teacher meetings – not necessarily of the whole team – are often more effective.

Exhibitions of all areas of work and discussions between teachers and with students are the most valuable methods of evaluation.

Resources in the form of photo-packs and slides are becoming available and should help to relate study in basic visual concepts. Too rigid a structure of lesson ideas should be guarded against as it could lessen the individual ideas of teachers and pupils.

Structure Pupils attend twice weekly (2 × 2, 40 min periods) and change material areas every 6/7 weeks.

Sequence THE SEQUENCE IS AS FOLLOWS:

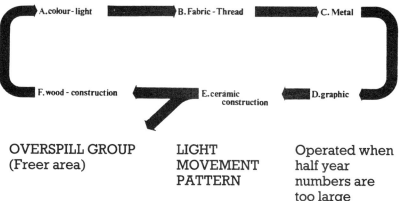

A. colour - light → B. Fabric - Thread → C. Metal

F. wood - construction ← E. ceramic construction ← D. graphic

OVERSPILL GROUP (Freer area)   LIGHT MOVEMENT PATTERN   Operated when half year numbers are too large

The sequence is deliberate. It is to lead from:

soft to hard;
2D surface to 3D surface;
colour to fabric;
etc.

211

EXAMPLE 2

Colour – light   Including simple picture-making – observed and imaginative.

Study **colour circle** in various ways.
Simple speedy developments.

Explore **limited colour** range and mixtures.

Colour $\begin{cases} \text{mixing/testing/matching} \\ \text{opacity/transparency/overpainting} \end{cases}$

within limitations of the classroom media.

Tones/tonal observation
Relationships – the 'fit' of colour on a surface.
Beware of too many lengthy exercises.
Try to incorporate exercises into picture-making – both **imaginary** and **observed**.

A strong 'visual' stimulus is needed for both observed and imaginative work (e.g. describing a known painting as the basis for imaginative picture-making). Observational studies are generally more successful.

Study **colour in nature** (mixing/matching).

Show slides of appropriate paintings at any stage.

Use **drawing** wherever possible for preparatory studies, notes, ideas etc.

Fabric – thread   Pupils have just arrived from Colour/Light. See what work they have been doing. They should know about primary and secondary colours, subdued and near ranges of colour – contrasts and tones. Their pictorial work might help as themes for collage. Refer to pattern-making in the graphic area.

1 Colour revision – understanding of woven textiles
Using scrap/tailors' swatches – pull apart to understand nature and method of weaving. Re-lay flat and bunched on rectangles of card. Discuss and sort different groupings and sequences:

colour selection – mostly 'near' colours plus one contrasting;
pattern organization;
surface texture/pattern;
effect of light on raised surfaces.

Mount and display different categories.

2 Imagination – range of colour/materials/texture – space filling

Using scrap and 'found' material collections – cut, fray, tear pieces – again imposing colour limitation – stick and stitch fabric collage of a theme allowing for a feeling of movement and/or drama:

storms at sea/coast/Dartmoor etc. or
from drawing of surroundings/faces/figures etc.

Emphasize light/dark ranges. Include any 'flat' material – even newspaper if appropriate. Unrealistic colour will be used – detail can be stitched or embroidered by some students.

3 Printed pattern

Repeat pattern is built up – always kept as a whole – repeated units plus developed units, e.g.

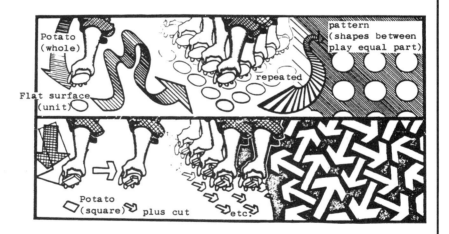

Cork/polystyrene. Develop using the same block for two-colour overprints on cheap paper and newspaper. Can be printed onto fabric pieces with dyes or bleach/paste negatives – make up into squares, scarves, ties etc.

Metal The main content of the work should be geared to the physical and material facilities of the Technical Studies Department. It is hoped that the use and exchange of experience will be maintained with other areas of the design

EXAMPLE 2

course. Teachers should understand the basic elements covered, e.g.

shape – control within a specific area, organic and/or geometric;

pattern – repetition of shape or texture marks, relationship and 'quality' of surface;

3D structure – developing 3D shapes from 2D surfaces in card and sheet metal, drawings in space with wire (either abstract or from simplification of natural forms), use clay and Plasticine to practise designs.

Encourage use of drawing – free or with geometric controls from actual objects and surfaces as source material for design ideas. Refer to pattern formation and developments in previous fabric area.

General procedures:

cutting and shaping of sheet materials;
surface treatments – incising, beating etc;
joining metals – soldering and brazing;
enamelling – refer to colour/light area for choice and use of colour;
polishing and finishing.

Graphic Concentrate upon mark-making/various drawing situations/simple 'graphic design' operations – some closely linked with picture-making in Colour/Light area.

Control of mark-making media:

pencil
pen
cut-spills
brush handles
charcoal
chalks etc.

Drawing and development from simple but interesting forms.
Imaginative themes.
Lighting – counterchange devices – simplification etc.

Print-making using simple blocks and materials – card, paper, vegetables.

All-over unit pattern making – printed or mixed media.
(Refer to Fabric area to reinforce pattern-making devices.)

Use sequential pattern building – 'stripe' or 'all-over' patterns.

Overprinting and reduction printing.

Ceramic – construction

Clay processes – mainly slab construction/coil construction.
Card/paper – cutting/folding/glueing/slotting etc. to be used
to extend experiences in clay.
This area should be closely related to other 3D areas (Wood
and Metal) – with similarities and distinctions, e.g.

constructed elements;
surface realization;
tool treatments; etc.

In pattern there should be a particular emphasis upon the
role of light/shade in the development of surface – the
natural development of 3D pattern into 2D pattern – use of
counterchange – use of controlled lighting to stimulate
discussion about and evaluation of patterns and forms.

Mark-making – tool marks/finger marks/incised/applied
treatments on tiles or similar slab constructions.
Coil or slab combinations/controlled beating/polishing of
surfaces.

Firing/glazing – use of simple glaze pigments.
Explore all possibilities of relating to and combining with
Wood area.

Wood – construction

Exercises using 3D materials as available: straws/cocktail
sticks/corks/polystyrene/wire/card/wood off-cuts/thin
strips/sheet/'found' materials.

Some areas already covered in Ceramics area can be
repeated or preferably combined with a two-teacher
'combined' introduction, e.g. modular structures,
interlocking forms, re-alignment of solid forms.

Studies of form and character of wood grain – tool
operations in respect of grain.

Use and control of main tools/correct handling/cross
cutting/vice positions etc. Shaping tools, measuring and
squaring.

Try to fuse inventive situations with woodworking
operations. This is a 'difficult' area – some operations will be
difficult for some pupils – allow scope and vary projects
according to the overall 'flavour' of the group.

EXAMPLE 3

EXAMPLE 3

Appearance and structure worksheets – art, textiles, woodwork and metalwork programmes (see page 204)

Stephen Disbrey   *Art and Craft Co-ordinator, Lower School, Paignton College*

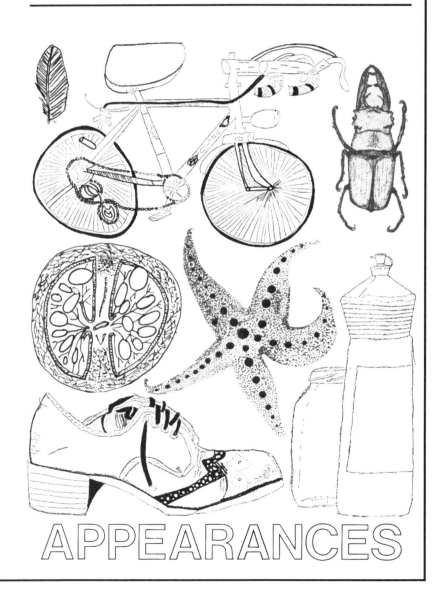

We want to know how things look and why they appear the way they do, in the natural and man-made world around us. This exploration can help us to express our feelings and ideas and enables us to create our own designs. Of course, we are looking at things all the time, but really to understand the appearance of something we have to focus our attention fully and inspect it carefully. Trying to record accurately, in the same way as a camera, can help us considerably. Unlike the camera, *we* are able to act 'selectively' or 'choose a particular area' in making our records. Thus, we may decide when looking at:

a flower – to concentrate on its colours;
a hedgehog – to concentrate on its texture;
a house – to concentrate on its shape.

The most important thing we do is to show our feelings about the objects, in addition to recording them and learning about them, in order to help us make our designs.

EXAMPLE 3

Stage one # Analyse and record

1 Choose one of the objects.

2 Explore your object by looking and handling it. What does it look like? Is it heavy, light, rough, smooth, dull, shiny, lumpy or bumpy? Does the shape remind you of anything? What do you think of it, do you like it? Write a brief description of what you have discovered.

3 Now really study it carefully, using a suitable 'focusing device'. Look for variations in shape, colour and texture. Record on paper all the information you collect as you go along. Here are some suggestions that might help:

Shape

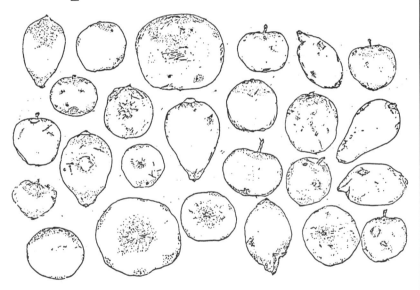

Make a drawing to record the shape of your object. Cut it out and stick it on black paper.
Is your object's shape regular or irregular?
Is it symmetrical or asymmetrical?
Can you use the shape to make a repeat pattern?
What happens when you overlap the shapes?

Stage one # Analyse and record

1 Choose one of the objects.

2 Explore your object by looking and handling it. What does it look like? Is it heavy, light, rough, smooth, dull, shiny, lumpy or bumpy? Does the shape remind you of anything? What do you think of it, do you like it? Write a brief description of what you have discovered.

3 Now really study it carefully, use a suitable 'focusing device'. Look for variations in shape, colour and texture. Record on paper all the information you collect as you go along. Here are some suggestions that might help:

Shape

As an example, a simple leaf and its potential could be an interesting starting point for a design.

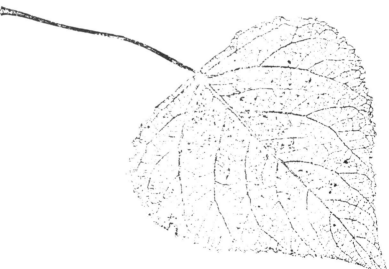

You can develop a shape by:

(a) changing the outer shape and size;
(b) changing the inner shape;
(c) cutting and replacing shapes;
(d) repeating the shape;
(e) adding other shapes;
(f) adding surface textures.

EXAMPLE 3

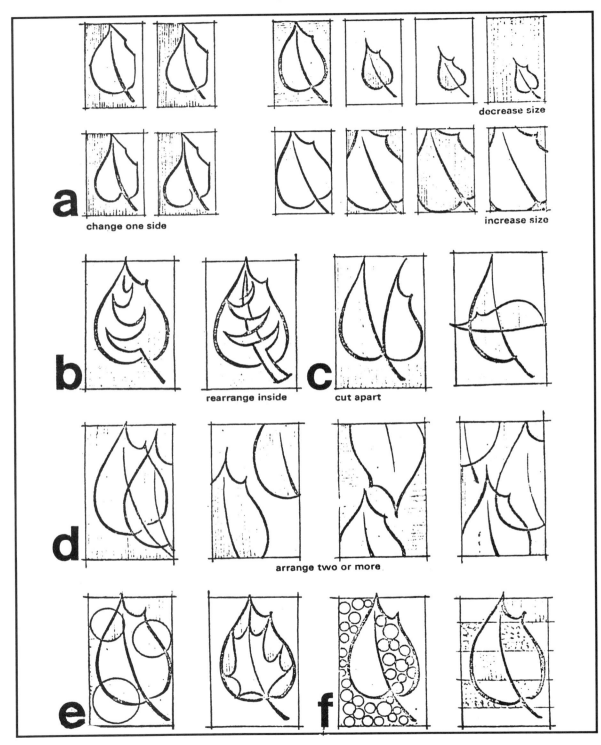

decrease size

increase size

a change one side

b rearrange inside c cut apart

d arrange two or more

e f

220

Stage two # Explore

Do not decide what the final design is going to be, yet explore with drawings.
Make as many drawings of the object as you can.
Draw the whole thing and draw small areas as seen through a magnifying glass.
If possible cut the object in half and make sketches of the cut pieces.
Find out and record what you discover about the surface.

Stage three # Develop

These discoveries in the form of drawings should be developed in a carefully thought out way as shown by examples (a), (b), (c), (d), (e), (f).

Stage four # Finished drawing

Produce a drawing showing chosen design (as agreed with the teacher). This drawing should represent as realistically as possible the design as it would look when made.

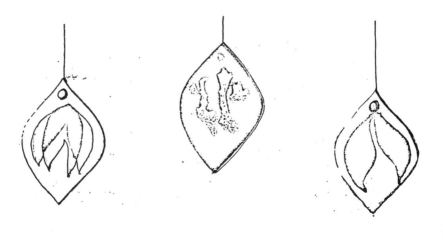

8 ART AND OTHER SUBJECTS

Art On Its Own?

The majority of secondary school art teachers are trained in colleges of art, and their post-graduate training may also take place in specialist centres. After five years of highly specialist training, it is sometimes something of a shock to the young art teacher to find that within a school he or she is simply a teacher of one subject amongst many and to find that art even has to be justified as a subject.

Secondary schools are almost universally subject-centred in their curriculum, and organization and claims for time, space and resources within the school are subject to negotiation and barter between departmental heads.

In these circumstances, you must be able to make a good case for the place of art in the curriculum in its own right. It also makes good educational sense for you to have some understanding of the relationship between art and other subjects, and how your concerns and interests in the teaching of children both match and complement the work of other subject teachers.

You will not further the cause of art teaching if – like some art teachers – you retreat into your own specialism and try to turn your art room into a little oasis in which the sensitive might take refuge from the philistines!

That there can be a useful working relationship between art and other subjects is admirably demonstrated in many primary and middle schools, where this is easily effected through the good class teacher who will teach his/her own class for the bulk of their curriculum. Integration of subjects is most noticeable in those primary schools committed to the philosophy of teaching from direct experience. When children are exploring their own real world, it is natural to respond to it and comment upon it through a variety of subject disciplines.

Although the organization of the secondary school timetable makes this kind of integration between subjects difficult, there are useful ways in which you can establish working relationships with other subjects. In doing this you may be able to enrich the work of your department in addition to extending the department's influence within the school.

Subject Relationships

Different subject disciplines can be related either through their working methods or through their content. For example, although the working methods used in the teaching of art and history are very different from each other they overlap when they are dealing with the development of certain cultures, particularly where this is evidenced mainly through the visual arts. There are obvious links between the working methods used in art and CDT departments, as in both subject areas there is an emphasis upon developing and realizing ideas through the handling of materials and techniques.

There are clearly very strong links between the teaching of art and English. Both subjects are a means of communication and expression. In much of our contemporary culture, word and image are often inter-related. In much prose and poetry, the visual world is expressed through the use of language – just as the use of language itself is an important focus for the children's visual perception of their world.

In recent years in primary schools, there has developed a good working relationship between art and science – especially in the environmental sciences, where the skills of observation and analysis acquired through drawing play an important part in the children's examination of natural and man-made phenomena.

At an informal level you can make good use of the work being done in other subjects in support of your work as an art teacher, simply by finding out *when* related work in other subjects is taking place. For example:

When do the children deal with the science of colour in their physics lessons?

When are the English staff planning a personal writing project with a year group on a theme that is relevant to their work in art?

When in geography do the children embark upon a detailed study of part of the local environment? etc.

Such occasions as these provide obvious starting points for shared work, where the skills and understanding developed in one subject may be used to support work in another.

There has been an attempt in a few schools to seek out common content through different subjects by requiring the staff to produce an outline curriculum map for one term, in order that common concerns might more easily be identified. In many schools there have been more formal attempts to link the work of different subjects, through the establishment of faculties or groups of related subjects. These have already been discussed in the previous chapter.

Faculty Groupings

The development of faculty structures within schools was closely linked to the emergence of comprehensive schools in the early 1960s, and with the need to provide management structures to cope with the needs of these new large schools. The development of art and design faculties, or 'creative design' faculties, was pioneered in Leicestershire and was to some extent determined by the decision to house practical subjects in one teaching block, since they all required similar services. Through these arrangements,

teachers of art, CDT and home economics were expected to come together under the general umbrella of 'design education'.

Although art teachers and departments can have much to offer within a design based curriculum (after all the vast majority of designers are trained in art schools!), the placing of art within this group does exclude the art teacher from contact with other subjects that have equally useful links to offer. In contrast to this, there are many schools where art is identified as being one of the 'expressive' subjects and where it is linked in faculty groupings with the other arts of music, drama and dance. As a matter of convenience, physical education is sometimes included within this group! There is no doubt that the 'expressive arts' can work well together and that it doesn't require a formal faculty grouping of this kind to ensure that they do.

Example 1 illustrates how the arts teachers in one school make good use of those occasional opportunities to link and relate their work. An important supporting element here is the good use that the arts departments make of informal liaison with the English department and how the use of language is seen as being a major co-ordinating element within their work.

Another important shared concern is in the emphasis within these arts departments upon teaching children through experiences that are real and meaningful to them and that are rooted in the child's real world – in contrast to so much else within the school curriculum that is concerned with teaching about the world at second hand.

A similar emphasis upon using the real world as a vehicle for arts teaching is illustrated in Example 2, where the teachers of art, music and drama in this school have used an exploration of the familiar sights and sounds of their small market town as the basis for the children's work in the arts.

In order to generate successful work across the arts, teachers of art, music and drama do have to recognize essential differences between the arts, as well as those things they have in common.

223

The most important differences lie within the relationship between the art form and action and evidence in the real world. Drama is the activity that is closest to action in the real world. In drama, children can recreate very quickly things and experiences that are immediate and real to them. At the other extreme, music is the form of expression that is most distant from the real world – it is the most abstract of the arts, and ideas in music are more likely to be expressed through the pure form of sounds rather than through recall or illustration of the world. The visual arts occupy a position somewhere between drama and music – they can be used to recall the world of everyday experience through visual images – they can also be used to communicate through a language of abstract symbols as in music.

The arts operate very differently to each other in the classroom – response through drama can be very immediate and it is essentially a group activity. As in music the product is transient – it is heard or seen but cannot be recalled unless it is recorded. Response through art or language is both more individual and more permanent. The picture, the poem, the story, the artefact – once produced it can be shared with others long after its emergence.

It is for these reasons that combined work in the arts is best realized through a positive linking, rather than through attempts to integrate them as though they were all similar ways of working. Where the arts work well together tends to be in those schools where teachers of art, music and drama recognize that they can provide experiences within their art form that can be built upon and extended through another art form.

In any combined arts work, the choice of theme is crucial since it has to allow for responses through the different art forms that may range from descriptive to symbolic. Some arts teachers have found that themes based on the use of polarities, e.g. familiar/strange, order/chaos, growth/decay etc. work particularly well, because they provide a structure for the work without limiting its content too closely.

Within expressive arts faculties – as in those centred around the concept of design – in planning the work of the team, it is essential to allow sufficient time for the individual arts to pursue their own concerns. There are basic skills and concepts in all the arts that have to be learnt and practised and without which combined work of any quality is unlikely to emerge. A useful pattern developed in some schools where the arts are grouped together is for the arts to work separately for two thirds of the year and to come together for combined work for two separate half-term projects.

In any combined work – in whatever combination of subjects – the sharing is essential as it is only through such public demonstration that the children are enabled to see the connections and common principles that may link the work that they have been doing in different studios and workshops.

The decision to place art within a design or expressive arts grouping within a school seems to indicate a particular view of the function of art within the school curriculum – that art is either more to do with designing and making things, or with expressing personal ideas and feelings. Since art is quite clearly to do with both, either grouping has some limitations in that it tends to exclude the art teacher from easy access to colleagues he may well wish to work with. In this sense, the larger faculty grouping of all the practical and aesthetic subjects under the umbrella of 'creative arts' or 'creative studies' can allow for more flexible working between art and those subjects with which there has traditionally been useful contact.

Whether you work in a single subject department, or in one of the variously titled multi-disciplinary faculties, you will need to look for ways to make sense of your subject in relation to others – not only to ensure that there is no unnecessary overlap of content in an already overcrowded curriculum, but also to seek the common ground that can help children to make better sense of their learning as they shuttle from one subject to another.

EXAMPLE 1

Working together – from the arts at Vincent Thompson High School

A description of the way that arts teachers in one school work together informally and make useful connections between their subjects (see pages 223–4).

Although there is no formal relationship between the arts subjects at Vincent Thompson High School – in terms of faculty structures or timetabling – there are useful and informal links between the arts that have developed through shared interests between subject teachers. As teachers of art, music, drama and English, we respect and value the specialist concerns we each have and recognize that each art form has its own language of discourse and exclusive ways of working with children. We also share some common attitudes as to the function of the arts in the sharpening and extension of children's perceptions. Out of this respect for each other's work and recognition of shared values there has grown, informally and over a number of years, a relevant and useful pattern of arts work in the school and one that is seen to be effective in the general education of children.

In the lower school, art and drama are timetabled as part of a 'creative arts' pool, which includes the full range of creative and practical subjects, with the exception of music. Here, art and drama have the advantage of being timetabled in small teaching groups of 18–20 pupils, which allows for close personal attention to the needs of individual children. Music is timetabled separately and in regular weekly modules throughout the lower school, and 'personal' writing plays a significant part in the pattern of English teaching.

The arts are popular within the option system for examination courses in the upper school, and the great majority of fourth- and fifth-year pupils are continuing to work in one aspect of the creative arts until they leave school.

Common elements Two major elements are common to the work in the different arts areas. We all place considerable emphasis upon the use of language as an essential core of arts teaching.

225

EXAMPLE 1

Drama, already rooted in action, thought, emotion, character and human relationships, offers many opportunities for the study of language . . . at all levels it is concerned with understanding and communication between individuals. Art will help the child to organize his seeing, what he perceives and how he expresses himself and his ideas. Discussion and verbalization about work between the teacher and individual children leads to self evaluation and criticism which are reinforced through group participation in the making of judgements. Music is a natural link to many areas of knowledge – it can complement and enhance language and often transcends it. Poetry, drama and fiction are surely the end product, the final fruition of language. We do not teach children English just to enable them to fill in forms or to absorb facts, but to develop their thinking and intuitive processes so that they can grow and change towards perception.

We also have a common view in seeing the arts as being primarily concerned with teaching children through experiences that are real and meaningful to them and that are rooted in the child's real world – in contrast to so much else in the curriculum that is concerned with teaching about the world at second hand. We believe that imagination is an extension or reconstruction of reality – that children write, paint, improvise, interact and make music more meaningfully when they are exploring ideas, concepts and situations that they have directly experienced. We make considerable use in our work of existing art forms and believe that by relating the children's work to the world of literature, music, fine art and theatre, we help to extend the children's horizons and their understanding of other people's perceptions. The music-making in the first two years is essentially practical, concerned with making and using sound. Listening to existing musical form is also used as the basis for the children's exploration of similar or related musical ideas. The work in art is based consistently upon examination of the real world, both of the environment and of the children's own view of themselves and their place in the world. In both English and drama, there is a concern to ensure that children's response through action and language is based upon encounters that have real meaning. A wide range of stimulus and source material is used to support this concern. In the arts, the direct experience of 'doing' or 'becoming' has the unparalleled quality, affiliation and understanding that no other group of subjects can offer.

We believe that this consistency of attitude between arts teachers ensures that the children see and use the arts as natural forms of expression that are essentially useful and relevant to their learning.

Specialist concerns

In addition, the arts pursue their own separate and specialist concerns – in music and art with the acquisition of the formal language of mark- and sound-making that is the essential basis for more complex and personal expression in these art forms. In drama, more than in any other of the arts, there is considerable emphasis upon the social values that may be achieved through engaging in an arts activity.

Drama is essentially a group activity and for that reason relies heavily upon group and social interaction. The use of role play within drama allows children to use 'the mask' to re-enact and come to terms with their relationships with their environment and with their friends.

Through role play, young people are enabled to question critically and constructively their position within the school and their social environment and to come to terms with the views and concerns of others.

Working together

There are occasions when the work in one of the arts overlaps and supports work in the other arts. This happens frequently in the use in each of the arts of forms and processes that are widely used in the teaching of one of the other arts. In English teaching there is considerable use made of source material that is visual and aural – pictures, puppets, classical and popular music and story 'telling' as opposed to reading. The work in art is frequently reinforced by writing and interaction. In music there is much use of dramatic and literary forms – listening to the 'Danse macabre' may lead to story telling and then back to the making of music to 'tell' the story.

Interaction between the arts occurs naturally in the joint work the arts departments contribute to a formal production, as in the recent production of Capek's 'The life of the insects', when some of the best improvised music-making of the year took place in percussion response to rehearsals of scenes from the play, for which the art department contributed scenery and properties.

There have been some informal experiments in co-operative teaching between the arts, as in the exploration

EXAMPLE I

of common themes between the art and English departments where, for two or three weeks, one year-group will work on a particular concept in all their art and English lessons, with a natural use of common source material and some ebb and flow of ideas between visual and language exploration. The paintings and poems that grew from a recent joint project on 'Dreams' also provided the basis for some imaginative work in music where the children made sound tapes to accompany the exhibition of the 'dream' theme. Similarly, the common exploration in art and English of the notion of 'faces and identity' led to strong supporting work in drama.

Summary   We believe that the arts flourish at Vincent Thompson because we have common concerns and aims and that these help to strengthen our individual contributions as arts teachers. We also wish to acknowledge the supportive nature of the school, and the help and encouragement given to the arts by senior members of staff. The arts enrich the life of the school in obvious and demonstrable ways – through the presentation of concerts, plays, exhibitions, events and publications.

In their presentation of opportunities for children to encounter the realities of their own world through description, communication and personal response, the arts contribute significantly to the quality of learning throughout the school and to the balance and meaning of the curriculum.

Margaret Payne
Anne Richards
Norman Schamforth
Sara Vernon

EXAMPLE 2

The sights and sounds of Axminster

Worksheets designed for a second-year group who were to explore parts of their local environment in support of a combined arts project. The worksheets suggest starting points for collecting information and evidence about things within the environment that could generate work in art, music and drama. The children used the drawings, notes and recordings made in this survey as the basis for six weeks' work across the arts.

EXAMPLE 2

THE TOWN   Site (1)

The Carpark of 'The George Hotel'...

Make notes of, and describe,

a) Sounds, cars, people, conversations (apart from those of your group), cries, shouts, calls, loud and soft sounds, far and near, human and mechanical sounds

Splut, bang!

The George Hotel

Whoof... Whoof...

...Scree--ee-ech

b) Look for gaps and openings, what can you see through archways and gate ways. Observe these from as many different angles as possible:- Describe and compare these!

Observe and record patterns, texture. Make notes in detail of all the vehicles in the car park; describe the age, colour, make, registration number, condition, etc.

Imagine the George Hotel 100 years ago. Who would work there? Describe the life of one of the employees of the Inn. Why do people visit the Inn? Who may be staying there now and where do they come from?

THE STATION AND STATION YARD.

Sounds

What sounds would you normally associate with a railway station?

Describe in your own words, the sound of a train as it approaches, stops and departs.

How would the sound of a modern station differ from that of a station 50 years ago?

Sights

RAILWAY BRIDGE - look through this and along the track until it vanishes into the distance. Record how the track appears to get smaller.

Record patterns and decoration used on the station

Draw details of the things that you would find only on a station

What do people look like when they are waiting? What are they doing? Is it busy or quiet.

Note - horizontals, verticals, town and countryside, rest and speed.

If a train arrives, describe how things change and what happens.

Describe different types of people.

Why are people travelling? Ask questions.

How do those waiting behave? How do those arriving behave?

Does the arrival of numbers of nameless, voiceless people in a metal container have any similarity with other situations you can think of?

EXAMPLE 2

THE STATION AND STATION YARD (contd.).

Explore the old sheds and structures behind the station. Record textures and contrasts in tone and pattern.

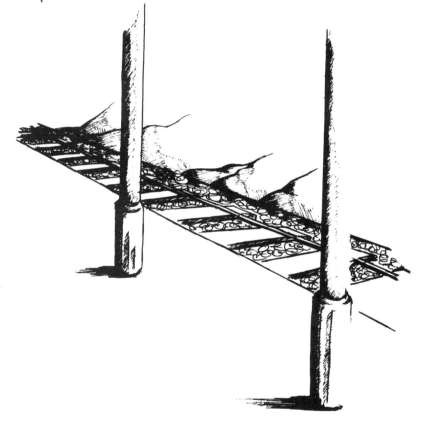

9 RECORD KEEPING AND ASSESSMENT

The Need for Record Keeping and Assessment

All schools require teachers to make a regular assessment of the work of individual children in all subjects. In most schools, there is a set pattern or timetable which determines at what point in each year children have to be graded, reported upon, examined and marked.

The first things you are likely to be given, as a new teacher in a new school, are the register, the mark book and the record book! In many schools you will regularly be asked to pin down the achievements of children to one grade for effort and one for attainment, yet very often there has been very little discussion about just what is meant by 'C' for effort or '3' for achievement. Many art teachers would argue that it is virtually impossible to evaluate or assess children's work in art in the same terms that other subjects are assessed. They might use the standard excuse 'that the process is more important than the product', and by implication assume that you cannot assess the process.

There are major differences between art and many other subjects. Art does not rely so much upon the acquisition of a certain body of know-ledge as is so evident in such subjects as history and physics. There are fewer certainties in art – in such subjects as mathematics and science, many things can be said to be right or wrong – in art we are more concerned with appropriate responses than with right answers. Nevertheless, even those art teachers who deny the possibility of assessment do continuously assess their pupils' work through their talk with the children, through their responses to the children's work, through choosing to display certain children's work and not others' etc. There is certainly much more evidence of continuous negotiated assess-ment in the work of a good art department than may be seen in many other departments. The very nature of the subject requires a consistent and progressive interplay between teacher and pupil, as the child moves through the school and, with the acquisition of skills and confidence, begins to want to use his or her skills in an increasingly personal way.

It may be difficult to 'mark' art as other subjects are sometimes marked, and certainly it cannot be done within the same narrow criteria. The nature and range of the tasks we set children within art and design do require us to adopt a more flexible system of assessment than other subjects may require – it must be obvious that you cannot assess by the same criteria tasks as various as making a colour chart, modelling a figure in clay, illustrating a poem or painting a dream.

Monitoring and Record Keeping

The essential base for fair and accurate assess-ment of the children's work is in developing within your department an efficient system for monitoring the children's work as they progress through the first two or three years. This re-quires a more detailed system of record keeping than the standard series of grades or marks in a register – especially when, as in many schools, the children may be taught by several art teachers during their time in the lower school.

The obvious and most useful support for moni-toring children's work is for them to keep and maintain an individual folder of their own work, dating all work within the folder, so that at any time of the year it is possible to review with individual children what work they have done and in what order. It is also important to keep some work from year to year so that progress can be visibly seen and commented upon. Obviously children will want to discard work they find unsatisfactory as they progress through the school, and will want to take home work of which they are particularly proud. Despite these constraints, it is possible to retain at least enough work to mirror what has been achieved and what progress has been made. This retention of work is especially crucial as children pass from art teacher to art teacher at termly or yearly intervals.

You can also make sure that children keep and maintain a sketchbook or notebook – or a drawing book for their homework assignments – as useful supporting evidence for the studio work they complete in school.

In addition to keeping the work itself there is a variety of supporting strategies that all contribute to a better understanding by the children of what they have achieved as well as helping teachers to evaluate more precisely what the children have learnt through the process of making. Example I provides some useful descriptions of these. Assessment is supported by:

time for reflection;
sharing ideas and experience within the group;
discussions about further possibilities of the work;
personal records or diaries;
reinforcement of experiences through repetition;
etc.

Implicit here is the notion that children's self-evaluation of their own work is as important as the teacher's assessment. The ability of children to appraise their own work can only develop when you allow time and provide the structure for this to happen. Some of the strategies for generating appraisal through talk and interaction have already been discussed in Chapter 3.

If you allow children to record some of their observations and comments about their own work as part of the departmental system of record keeping, they become fully aware of the importance of their own decisions and conclusions in the forming of their work. There are a whole variety of ways in which a simple record card system can allow for children's self-appraisal to contribute to the monitoring of their work. Four types of record card are described in Example 2. Three of the four record cards require the art teachers concerned to attempt some simple assessment through grading on an A–E scale for both attainment and effort. It is obviously necessary to have a reasonably accurate notion of what is meant by 'B' for effort and 'C' for attainment, which does mean undertaking detailed discussion about what the gradings mean in terms of the children's performance. Example 3 is a useful example of the assessment criteria that can emerge from discussion of this kind. These criteria were agreed as the basis for termly assessment within a creative arts faculty, including art, home economics and CDT, where the movement of children from one area to another at half-termly intervals did require that some care was needed to make sure that different subject teachers were using similar criteria in their assessment of the children's work.

Careful monitoring of the children's work becomes even more important if you are working in a large department or faculty and the children are being taught art and design by several teachers within the same academic year.

The notes in Example I make specific reference to the close link between evaluation and project planning:

> Assessment is dependent upon having clearly defined aims and strategies established before the outset of a project. Only by having reference points can we hope to match achievement with objectives. Evaluation therefore becomes an integral part of project planning: what we have done, how they respond, what they think they have achieved, what the standard of work was like

and how do you know they want to carry on, form the discussion points for the development of projects.

This link between syllabus and project planning and assessment is discussed in greater detail in the following section.

Assessment Models

The way in which you assess children's work in art will be determined by the curriculum model you use as a framework for your work with children, which is itself shaped by the aims and objectives that support your work. If, for example, you construct an art curriculum around the model suggested by Maurice Barrett (see pages 11–12), then your assessment objectives will be determined by his description of the three elements that shape the making of art:

The personal or conceptual element	How effectively does a child show a personal response to an idea, theme or other stimulus?
The technical element	How well does the child select and control materials and resources appropriate to his or her intention?
The visual element	How effectively does the child use and compose elements of visual form, e.g. line, tone, colour etc?

If in your planning of the art curriculum you construct a syllabus which is shaped by the different kinds of aims described in Chapter 1 (pages 11–12), your assessment objectives will be determined by these four categories of aims: aesthetic, perceptual, technical and personal.

In attempting to assess the work of younger children, it is almost certainly sufficient to work to a very simple assessment model based on what thinking, looking and making skills are evident within the work.

In Example 4, Michael Stevenson has constructed a very useful assessment model for non-specialist teachers in primary schools. In considering the way in which assessment might be determined by the kind of thinking processes used by children in the making of a painting or artefact, he has arrived at an assessment profile that is valuable to both the general teacher and the specialist teacher of art.

It is interesting to compare this profile with that in Example 5, which has been designed for use in a department where the children are taught by four different art teachers during their first three years in the school, where it is obviously necessary to keep a careful record of the children's work as they move from one teacher to another.

Despite the differences in language and terminology, the two profiles give similar weight to assessing, on the one hand, such straightforward things as the visual and technical skills that have been achieved and, on the other, the more complex matter of how well the children move from initial observations, through selection, towards some kind of personal statement or expression.

The primary school profile interestingly leaves room for assessment of the children's expression of ideas, both verbally and visually, which raises the inevitable question of how you take account of those aspects of the children's work in art that are not evident in the work itself. Although much of what the child has achieved will be evident in the work, there are some perceptions and responses that will contribute to the making but which may not necessarily be present in the final form.

The kind of talk and perceptions that are realized through discussions both with teacher and friends within the group is one quality that may be an important by-product of practical work in the art room. Others might include:

how well the child works co-operatively with other children;

how much determination is shown in overcoming difficulties;

how much the child is influenced by the work of other pupils – and of other artists;

etc.

Within the school or department where the assessment is internal to the school, such important qualities as these can be taken into account in the assessment of the children's work. Although they may be difficult to record through formal grading, they can be referred to and commented upon within the written reports upon the children's progress that have to be made at least once in every academic year.

Where the children's work has to be subject to external assessment – as in the examinations at 16-plus – it becomes very difficult to include within the assessment of children's work anything that is not present within the work itself or revealed through the preliminary studies, writing and research notes that support the work.

The National Criteria for Art and Design for the GCSE examination accept this as an inevitable consequence of presenting children's work for external assessment. The GCSE Boards Joint Council for 16-plus National Criteria states in its paper on criteria for art and design:

> The aims given below set out the educational purposes of following a course in art and design for all potential candidates. They include reference to a number of attributes and qualities which cannot or should not be assessed for examination purposes but which, nevertheless, form an essential part of any art and design course. In this respect the aims differ from the assessment objectives which all refer to qualities and competences to be assessed.

The aims and assessment criteria for the GCSE examination are listed in Example 6.

Many art teachers will regret this compromise, but it is part and parcel of the 16-plus examinations system, which is almost entirely based upon assessing children's performance at the end of a two-year course. At least in art and design, a healthy proportion of the assessment is based upon course work and upon evidence of the student's thinking through preliminary notes, studies and drawings.

There is a significant difference between the system of assessment in schools for art and design and that present in further and higher education in art. In further education as in, for example, foundation and B Tec. courses, the student is assessed throughout the course, and every piece of work or project undertaken during the course contributes to the overall assessment. This does mean that courses in further education and their content have to be forward planned in much more detail than is required in schools. A pattern of continuous assessment must be established that reflects the course detail.

This method of course construction, and the use within it of differentiated assessment for different parts of the course, can have interesting implications for work in schools that both leads into and overlaps with work in further education.

Differentiated Assessment and Course Structure

Since the nature of art teaching and of learning through art allows for a much more natural and personal means of assessment to operate than in many other subjects, it does seem reasonable to take this into account when planning projects and courses. A characteristic of good art teaching is the way the art teacher sets up a continuous dialogue with individual children about their work as it progresses. This dialogue will consist of a mixture of exchanges between teacher and child: some searching, some encouraging, some prodding and some straightforward exchange of information. All this adds up to a form of continuous negotiated assessment in which the child responds through his or her own making to the problems and possibilities presented. It is also clear that the content of this exchange varies significantly from task to task and changes in its emphasis as children pass through the school.

When younger children are drawing from observation, the exchange is a fairly simple one and will be concerned with ways of making different kinds of marks, ways of measuring, ways of looking carefully:

Try using the chalk over the charcoal.
Where will you need to use the pencil lightly?
Does it really curve as much as that?
Can you see all of that ear?

The dialogue will change in emphasis depending upon the task and so will the balance of assessment that is implicit in this kind of exchange. Dialogue about drawing is mainly about looking – technical matters are supportive to the looking. Dialogue about making a pinch-pot in clay is mainly about technical matters. Dialogue about making a drawing of a dream is mainly about notions.

If and when the children's work has to be formally assessed, and real marks entered into a mark book, it will make much more sense to the children if they know how the grade or mark was arrived at – which aspects of the work were most successful. If a pupil has spent the best part of three hours making a drawing of a still-life group, more response than C+ or six out of ten is deserved! Assessment of such a task will flow more naturally if both the introduction to the task and group appraisal at the end focus upon those different elements within such a drawing:

How well is space described within the drawing?
Do the objects appear to be solid?
Are the materials used sensitively to explain the surfaces?
Has a variety of weight of pencil been used?
Has an interesting aspect of the group been chosen?
How well is it arranged within the page?

Is this a better drawing than the last one you made?

Formal assessment of the children's work need not become unduly artificial as some teachers fear, as long as within the structure of the work and through the discussion and appraisal about it the children are fully informed about what is being assessed and why. As they progress through the school, it becomes more and more important to involve the children in their own assessment of their work. This can be encouraged by the way in which projects are set and courses are introduced to them.

Example 7 describes a course structure that has been designed for use with fourth- and fifth-year pupils working towards external examination. The balance of work over the two years is carefully mapped out and detailed consideration is given to the differentiated assessment between each project. The students are given each of the project sheets in turn, together with supporting work and enquiry sheets, and they know in advance how each project is going to be assessed and what weight of assessment is given to each aspect of the work. The projects may be given in different sequence depending on the response of the group and the varying abilities within the group.

In this school, as in other schools, the art teachers have commented upon the improvement in the level of motivation and understanding amongst their pupils when the curriculum is opened up to them in this way, so that they know more specifically what they are working towards.

This way of working with older pupils, which is more familiar within further education, can do much to help them to see the overall structure and purpose of their work, week by week and term by term. It may also help to overcome some of the mystery and confusion that sometimes shrouds the assessment of children's work in art.

EXAMPLE I

EXAMPLE I

Introductory notes to the expressive arts syllabus, Queen
Elizabeth School, Crediton

Jackie Ross   *Head of Expressive Arts Department*

General guidelines for assessment within an expressive arts
department that includes art, drama, music and textiles. These
notes refer to the variety of ways that children's work is assessed,
in addition to the formal grading of their work (see pages 233–4).

The experience

When planning projects and schemes of work, we aim
deliberately to provide time or space during a session or
number of sessions for some of the following:

Opportunities for:
time/space for their assessment of their work;
pride and a sense of achievement in their work;
quiet individual reflective work;
use of expressive arts sketchbook/diaries;
sharing of ideas/experiences within the group;
relevant reference to culture and civilization/place in history;
discussion/awareness of further possibilities of the work;
reading and gleaning from non-verbal material;
wondering, conjecture and imagining;
detailed observational drawings and notation;
development of manipulative skills;
opportunity of independent work;
sharing of work within the group and/or school.

Every project, session or part of session should have:
a deliberate focus area;
a conscious balance of activities.

After a number of projects pupils should have:
a personal record of what they have done (diaries);
a number of experiences;
a folder of work;
a reinforcement of experiences by repetition;
the ability and interest to develop projects further.

The strategies   Strategies need to be carefully matched to activities. The use of role play as an all-involving beginning, designed to achieve group identification with a new situation, is very different from quiet individual problem setting which looks for individual absorption and concentration.

The theme of the project, the focal points, the provision of opportunities and the strategies we use are all inter-dependent. The breakdown into compartments is a useful way of examining our teaching and their learning.

Assessment   Assessment is dependent upon having clearly defined aims and strategies established before the outset of a project. Only by having reference points can we hope to match achievement with objectives. Evaluation, therefore, becomes an integral part of project planning. What we have done, how they respond, what they think they have achieved, what the standard of work was like and how you know they want to carry on, form the discussion points for the development of projects.

The children's assessment of their own achievement is an element that should not be overlooked. Finding the right moment and the appropriate form for the expression of thoughts and feelings should be established from the first year. Reflecting on experiences and learning to value their own work is important and contributes to the longer term aim of developing more discriminating young people.

A record of the pupils' work will be found in their folders and expressive arts books. We need to ensure that we keep records of things not found in their books – for example, contribution to, and ability to work in groups, and whether they have a particular feel for visual, practical or mechanical areas of work. These are, in fact, all those things we need to know when compiling profile reports.

Among the things we are looking for are:

high standards of work;
a continuous working process;
an independent and responsible attitude;
self-assessment and evaluation.

These should be encouraged through the careful use of personal sketchbooks, diaries and folders, as well as through group sharing and individual discussion with staff.

Folders provide the opportunity to look back, to take pride in a year's work, to develop work at a later stage in the

EXAMPLE I

overall scheme and to 'get out and continue with work through breaks and lunchtimes'. Work from as many areas as is practicable can be kept in folders. They can stay with pupils from one half-year's subjects to the next, offering opportunities for cross-referencing and reminders.

Sketchbooks/diaries, which this year will be introduced at the start of the year by art, expressive arts, textile or design staff, should become an important part of the creative arts as well as the expressive arts course. They should show evidence of the working/exploring/thinking process and can be used for notes which reflect 'what we have done today' as well as the normal drawing, notation and homework.

EXAMPLE 2

Examples of record cards

Tony Preston	*Head of Arts Department, Estover School, Plymouth*
Peter Riches	*Head of Creative Studies Department, Eggbuckland School, Plymouth*
Stephen Disbrey	*Art and Craft Co-ordinator, Lower School, Paignton College*
Tony Littlewood	*Head of Creative Arts Faculty, Holsworthy School*

NAME	FORM		GROUP		Design – ART			
	OBSERVATIONAL	IMAGINATIVE	3 DIMENSIONAL	TEXTILES
	A B C D E	A B C D E	A B C D E	A B C D E
EFFORT				
ATTAINMENT				
QUALITY OF IDEAS				
INTEREST SHOWN				
UNDERSTANDING OF CONCEPTS				
PRESENTATION OF WORK				
TECHNICAL SKILL				
PERSONAL ORGANISATION				
ADDITIONAL COMMENTS				

EXAMPLE 2

ART PROJECT RECORD	NAME		TUTOR GROUP	
	ART GROUP	AREA		
	THEME		DATE	

IDEA(S):

ORGANIZATION (WRITE/DRAW METHODS BELOW):

MATERIALS:

COMMENTS: | STUDENT | | STAFF | | GRADES |

| | SKETCH BOOK | FOLDER | EFFORT | ACHIEVEMENT |

CREATIVE STUDIES/ART/YEARS 4 & 5

DATE OF ENTRY [1]	SURNAME	CHRISTIAN NAMES						SHEET NO

| DATES OF WORK PERIOD [4] | STARTING POINT | DESCRIPTION OF THE ACTIVITY [5] | [2] 1 | 2 | 3 | 4 | 5 | |

INTEREST [6 7] SUCCESS [8]

PUPIL'S COMMENTS

TEACHER'S COMMENTS [9]

[10]

243

EXAMPLE 2

DESIGN RECORD — MAJOR PROJECT

NAME				FORM	
PROJECT					NO
DATE SET		DEADLINE		COMPLETE	

STAGES	MAX. %	PUPIL MARK	STAFF MARK	COMMENT
Research depth breadth				
IDEAS range originality relevance				
DEVELOPMENTS trials–models –variations				
REALISATION sensitivity–techniques effectiveness				
EVALUATION appreciation				
TOTAL % CSE/GCE equiv.	100			

A/E

INVOLVEMENT		
DRAWING/OBS		
WRITING		
H/W INITIATIVES		

SELF ASSESSMENT

RECOMMENDATIONS

           STAFF

GCE/CSE	ABC/1 = 80% +	4 = 20% +
EQUIVALENT	2 = 60% +	5 = 10% +
ESTIMATES	3 = 40% +	0 = 9% −

EXAMPLE 3

Criteria for assessment of second- and third-year pupils,
St Thomas High School, Exeter

Descriptions of assessment criteria produced by a group of art, home economics and CDT teachers working together within a creative arts faculty. These descriptions provide useful guidelines for teachers who are required to assess children's work at regular intervals within the standard convention of awarding A–E grades for effort and achievement.

Within the creative arts faculty, second- and third-year pupils are assessed for their attainments (grades A–E) and for their attitude and effort (grades 1–5). The following criteria are used in order to assess which grades should be awarded.

Attainment

A Highly creative, fixed long-term retention, capable of extending boundaries of a problem/situation. Showing a high level of skills and excellent control of media for age group. Able to conceive a whole task from initial idea to completion.

B Good retention when occasionally reinforced. A good standard of creativity, competent control of media. Able to work independently.

C Medium term retention (lesson to lesson). Creative but incapable of extending boundaries on an individual level. Requires guidance.

D Showing minimal creativity. Little retention from lesson to lesson and needs constant revision and individual attention.

E No understanding of concepts. Little or no retention. Very poor co-ordination and media control.

Attitude/effort

1 Highly motivated, seeking involvement, helpful and respected by peers. Keen to raise standards. Very dependable.

EXAMPLE 3

2 Reasonably well motivated, self-reliant, sometimes initiating action, usually contributes, concerned. Usually dependable.

3 Not always interested, rarely showing necessary initiative. Dependent, needs to be more active, needs supervision.

4 Rarely interested, seldom initiates anything, unco-operative at times. Not sufficiently concerned to ensure quality, needs perpetual supervision.

5 Never interested, never initiates any action, disruptive. Shows no concern over performance, requires constant close individual supervision.

EXAMPLE 4

An assessment framework for use in primary schools

Michael Stevenson   *Curriculum Development Leader, Visual Arts, Manchester LEA*

An assessment model for use in primary schools which is based upon the thinking processes used by children as they move from initial observation, through selection, towards personal statement and expression.

Process of involvement used by children

1 *Perception* – the exploration and examination of the world around us through the medium of the senses.

2 *Selection* – the selection of one aspect of that which we perceive which stimulates us.

3 *Recognition* – the recognition of the idea, feeling, solution etc. which the stimulus generates.

4 *Expression* – the expression of the recognized response in some appropriate form.

Art teaching

(a) *Materials and techniques* – the development of each child's ability to handle an increasing range of materials with growing confidence and skill.

(b) *Perception* – the development of each child's capacity to see the world around him with increasing degrees of depth and analysis, as well as his capacity to take delight in what he sees.

(c) *Visual language* – the knowledge of and ability to use the basic vocabulary of line, shape, colour, tone, texture, space and pattern from which pictures are made, as well as an awareness of the way in which artists in our own and other cultures have used them.

(d) *Creativity* – the fostering and encouragement of each child's capacity to produce original ideas and solutions to problems which reflect his individual uniqueness.

247

EXAMPLE 4

Primary art checklist

This checklist is designed to structure our observations of children working. Much of the information can only be obtained through dialogue with the individual child. The simple yes/no response will indicate to teachers areas of concern which the teacher will take action on.

Yes = The child needs no action in this area at this time.

No = The child is encountering difficulties which the teacher needs to investigate further, make decisions about, and take action upon.

Sensory explorations

Do the children readily explore their environment through the medium of their senses?
Does their exploring enable them to extract accurate information about their environment?
Do they trust in the information they receive through their senses?
Do their observations result in a more 'finely tuned' perception of the qualities which they observe?

Selection/recognition

Do the children have an idea/feeling/response?
Do I know clearly what they are trying to say?
Is the quality of their ideas appropriate to their maturational/intelligence levels?
Are the ideas their own? an amalgamation? an extension? an imitation? a copy?
Is the idea appropriate to the problem/situation?

Expression

Does their work satisfy them in terms of what they set out to do?
Are their means of expression appropriate to what they are trying to do?
Have the children chosen their materials with consideration for what they will do?
Are the children demonstrating control over the materials they are using?
Can they justify their work in terms of what they intended to do?
Can they suggest alternative solutions?
Do they recognize the discoveries and statements they have made?
Are they satisfied with their results?
Has the work triggered further responses/ideas which they want to develop?

ART RECORD

Name   Class   Age   Date

	Well below norm	Below norm	Corresponds to agreed norm	In advance of norm	Well in advance of norm
PERCEPTION a) Visual b) Tactile					
PRODUCTION OF IDEAS FROM STIMULI					
EXPRESSIONS OF IDEAS a) Verbally b) Visually					
VISUAL LANGUAGE a) Colour b) Line c) Shape d) Pattern e) Tone f) Scale g) Synthesis					
TECHNICAL SKILLS (List media used) a) b) c) d) e) f)					

CREATIVITY	A copy of an existing idea	An imitation of stereotype	An amalgamation of other ideas	An extension of other ideas	Completely original
a) Ideas are usually					
b) End Products are usually					

EXAMPLE 5

Example 5

Assessment profile, years 1–3, Ilfracombe School

Malcolm Wilkinson
Colin Jacob

This assessment profile is designed to keep a record of the
children's work in the department where, during the first three
years, they will be taught by four different art teachers.

ILFRACOMBE SCHOOL	ART DEPARTMENT		ASSESSMENT RECORD			
NAME	TUTOR GROUP	Year 1	CLASS	Date of Entry		
		Year 2	HOUSE	Previous School		
		Year 3				

SUBJECT AWARENESS	Ability Grades	1 High Level	2 High Average	3 Average	4 Below Average	5 Low Level	
Expression							
Interpretation							
Perception							
VISUAL LANGUAGE							
Line							
Tone							
Colour							
Pattern							
Texture							
Form							
Space							
Composition							
TECHNICAL ABILITY							
Drawing							
Painting							
Printing							
Graphics							
Photography							
Pottery							
3D							
Textiles							
Attainment							
Effort							
Behaviour							
MERIT MARKS							
TEACHER							

EXAMPLE 6

National Criteria for art and design, aims and assessment objectives

GCSE Boards Joint Council for 16-plus National Criteria.

The aims of art and design

In the context of general education, the aims of art and design education are to stimulate, encourage and develop:

(a) the ability to perceive, understand and express concepts and feelings in visual and tactile form;

(b) the ability to record from direct observation and personal experience;

(c) the ability to form, compose and communicate in two and three dimensions by the use of materials in a systematic and disciplined way;

(d) the acquisition and understanding of technical competence and manipulative skills which will enable individuals to realize their creative intentions;

(e) experimentation and innovation through the inventive use of materials and techniques;

(f) intuitive and imaginative abilities, and critical and analytical faculties;

(g) the ability to identify and solve problems in visual and tactile form: to research, select, make and evaluate in a continuum;

(h) the ability to organize and relate abstract notions (ideas) to practical outcomes;

(i) awareness and appreciation of relationships between art and design and the individual within the historical, social and environmental context;

(j) the acquisition of a working vocabulary relevant to the subject;

(k) the individual's special aptitudes and interests and to foster and encourage confidence, enthusiasm and a sense of achievement;

(l) the understanding of economic considerations which might become limiting factors in the inventive use of materials and techniques.

EXAMPLE 6

The assessment objectives

Candidates will be expected to demonstrate the ability to:

(a) show a personal response to a stimulus, e.g. an idea, theme or subject;

(b) record from direct observation and personal experience;

(c) sustain a chosen study from conception to realization;

(d) work independently in realizing their intentions;

(e) analyse an idea, theme, subject or concept and to select, research and communicate relevant information and to make and evaluate in a continuum;

(f) select and control materials and processes in a systematic and disciplined way (taking account of considerations of costs as appropriate);

(g) synthesize ideas, impulse and feelings with materials, techniques and processes;

(h) use and compose visual elements, e.g. line, tone, colour, pattern, texture, shape, form, space.

EXAMPLE 7

A two-year course with built-in assessment points, Braunton School

Alan Phillips   *Head of Art Department*

This example includes only the work of the first four months of this two-year course.

Art – skill, especially human skill as opposed to nature; skill applied to imitation and design.
Fine arts (demanding mind and imagination).
A skill is more than knowing and more than knowing how. It is action too. A skill involves the application of knowledge to achieve some anticipated outcome. It needs the capacity and the will to act, as well as knowledge. Skill without knowledge is inconceivable, but knowledge without skill has a long sad history.
Knowledge implies understanding, not verbal knowledge of definitions.

I believe that designing and evaluating profile assessment methods cannot be conceived separately from the designing and assessment of the course, if you are to ensure inbuilt validity.

(a) General outline of aims.
(b) Design the scheme with *specific* plans and assessment points. (This does not mean it will be limiting, as each teacher uses his/her professional judgement, individual talent/style/skills within the general framework.)
(c) Test out model and document work produced, and evaluate profiles built up.

Avoid too much amorphous, sloppy jargon. The model needs to be clearly defined and highly detailed.

EXAMPLE 7

AIMS

(i)   To provide a clearly defined course for use as a model that
        covers the significant points of the criteria for
        assessment at 16+.

(ii)   To synthesise abstract language and ideas into a concrete
        form that transmits clear and unmistakeable information about
        the proposed model.

(iii)   To base the model framework on own experiences using tested
        projects that are conducive to learning whilst allowing other
        users (teachers/pupils) to do the same.

Sept ——————— 20 months ——————— June		ASSESSMENT →	PROFILES ←	SKETCH NOTE BOOKS
PROJECT BASES				
Acquisition of skill is to be encouraged. The skill is developed by the work not the work by the skill.	SKILLS TECHNIQUES	TIMES/POINTS TYPE) Process) and HOW) Product	Written by staff at the end of each PROJECT	Percentage of the final mark for NOTE and SKETCH BOOKS making these a compulsory element.
A. The activity of Self Expression: The individual's innate need to communicate his thoughts, feelings and emotions to other people	IMAGINATIVE EXPRESSIVE			
B. The activity of Observation: The individual's desire to record his sense impressions, to clarify his conceptual knowledge, to build up his memory, to construct things which aid his practical activities	OBSERVATION	MARK AND GRADE	Comment related to individual performances	
C. The activity of Appreciation: The response of the individual to the modes of expression which other people address or have addressed to him, and generally the individual response to values in the world of facts. The qualitative reaction to the quantitative results of activities A and B	HISTORY APPRECIATION	Continuous with SPECIALS submitted at particular points		

CRITERIA FOR ASSESSMENT

Applied Knowledge: (Experience and understanding of concepts)

The question to ask oneself. What has been learned?

Skills (i)   Both executive and descriptive skills.
       (ii)   Appropriateness, control and suitability of media.
       (iii) Thinking strategies and sense of planning necessary
              for effective creative performance.

Expressive and Creative abilities

        (i)   Elements of communication.

        (ii)   Personal involvement and/or feeling.

        (iii)   Originality (Newness for the person doing it).

        (iv)   Inventiveness and Enterprise.

These are the elements into which the work may be analysed or
viewpoints from which a work can be studied.

TWO YEAR COURSE WITH ASSESSMENT POINTS

Month One 20 marks	(i)	12 for Graphics Project excluding Notes, Homework research.
		Critical appraisal of the product by the group.
		Marked by the teacher.
	(ii)	5 for Drawing from Observation.
	(iii)	3 for Notes and Homework research.
		Individual pupil profiles started with the recording of these marks and comments on performance.

PROJECT ONE	GRAPHIC OR COMMERCIAL DESIGN
A good disciplined starter	Book Jacket, Programme Design, Record Sleeve, Badge, Poster, Logo, etc.

	INPUT	Introductory Talk Look at – Magazines, Shops, TV etc examples. Tightly Prescribed.
	TIME LIMIT	6 double periods. 3 weeks.
	SKILLS	Need to show they can work in an organised manner to develop their ideas.
		10% of Marks for the preliminary work and trials.
	ASSESS	(i) Communication 40%. (ii) Direct manipulation of materials 30%. (iii) Ability to work to a given completion date 20%.

PROJECT TWO	DRAWING FROM OBSERVATION Posed figures – seated standing
TIME LIMIT	2 Double periods. 1 week
ASSESS	(i) Layout 20%. (ii) Construction 40%. (iii) Proportion 40%.

COMMENTS

EXAMPLE 7

| Month Two 20 marks | (i) 6 for the following - Pupils to make notes during the Input session. Homework. Complete a short essay on ONE aspect of the slides shown with _their_ coloured copies of paintings and reproductions (cut outs). To be completed and handed in at the end of the month. |

(ii) 2 for Preliminary Studies and work.

(iii) 10 for Painting or Sculpture.

(iv) 2 for Display.

| PROJECT THREE | PICTORIAL COMPOSITION/3 DIMENSIONAL WORK |
| | FINE ART |

INPUT	Look at slides of paintings and sculpture. Ensure good content range. e.g. Portraits, still life, landscape, narrative, imaginative. Talk about Styles, Differences etc. Discuss and ask pupils to write preferences _with_ _reasons._
TIME LIMIT	7 double periods. 3½ weeks.
	5 titles given that echo the range. Pupils expected to research and then produce a PAINTING OR SCULPTURE based on their choice.
ASSESS	(i) Original and Interpretative work 30%. (ii) Personal Expression 40%. (iii) Skill 30%. After assessing have one double period for DISPLAY and CRITIQUE.

COMMENTS

256

Month Three 30 marks	(i) 10 marks for Applied Knowledge.
	(ii) 10 marks for Skills.
	(a) Both executive and descriptive.
	(b) Appropriateness, control and suitability of media.
	(c) Thinking strategies and sense of planning.
	(iii) 10 marks for Expressive and Creative Abilities.

PROJECT FOUR	PROJECT BASED ON THE LOCAL ENVIRONMENT
INPUT	1 Double period. A talk on the local environment. The visually interesting bits - background etc and then a sensory walk around the
	School } to make notes, produce quick Village } sketches etc.
	Homework - Make drawings of local environment.
TIME LIMIT	3½ weeks - 7 periods excluding the above.
	Using words/images or just images produce a piece of work with Braunton or your home village as the setting:- Story Illustration Comic Strip Painting, Map, Model etc.
	The essential requirement is to communicate aspects or facets of the local environment. The details gathered in initially (walk and homework) to act as starting points.
ASSESS	MAJOR PROJECT that contains all 3 analytical elements. Enter marks on profile and record individual development.

COMMENTS

EXAMPLE 7

Month Four	(i) 10 marks for one week project.	
30 marks This month's work to offset the earlier more PRESCRIPTIVE projects and allow a more free and imaginative approach.	(ii) 20 marks for project based on RESPONSES to PERSONAL CHOICE	
	PROJECT FIVE	SOUND RESPONSES
	TIME LIMIT	1 week - 2 double periods
	INPUT	Listen to music for 1 period. Make marks, notes, doodles. Period 2 arrange, make order of, organise. Final Double period to produce a coloured piece of work based on initial marks. (Time limit to prevent becoming precious)
	ASSESS	Mark - Communication and Expressive Qualities 50%. Layout 50%.
	PROJECT SIX	PERSONAL CHOICE
		Base your work on (a) A piece of music
		(b) A piece of writing { Poetry Prose
		(c) Coloured slides/photographs
		Respond by (i) Words (ii) Colours (iii) Symbols (iv) Doodles (v) Drawings (vi) Descriptive Images
		NOTEBOOK for working ideas, notes and studies.
		You must show clearly the development of your ideas and all preliminary studies will be included in the Assessment. You must mount and present your studies along with the finished piece of work.
	ASSESS	(i) Thinking Strategies (ii) Personal Involvement (iii) Inventiveness and enterprise COMMENT on to profile of the individual's performance. IMPORTANT on this one as a guide to tenacity and determination.
COMMENTS		

258

RESOURCES AND BIBLIOGRAPHY

Resources

Advisers

All local education authorities have an advisory service consisting of advisers (or inspectors) and advisory teachers or consultants. The majority of LEAs have a specialist adviser for art education who is responsible for supporting and monitoring work in art in the authority's schools and for developing a programme of in-service training in art education. In some authorities, an adviser will be responsible for both art and CDT, under the general heading of art and design. Where an authority does not have a specialist adviser for art education, it may nominate one of its general advisers to have an oversight of art education.

Artists in residence

Artists in residence in schools are sponsored through the Regional Arts Associations (see separate entry). The normal period of residency is for ten days, although longer periods of residence are occasionally available.

These residencies provide children with a rare opportunity to witness an artist at work, and in many schools a residency is used to generate teaching programmes related to the artist's work.

Enquiries about residencies should be made through your art adviser, or directly to your Regional Arts Association.

Arts Council

The Arts Council of Great Britain is the principal funding body for public sponsorship of the arts. Much of its work at local level is done through the RAAs. The Arts Council has an Education Unit which seeks to encourage closer co-operation between the professional arts and education at all levels, with a view to developing the knowledge, understanding and practice of the arts.

The Arts Council Educational Bulletin is produced each term and reports on a wide range of joint ventures. It is distributed to most schools via LEA internal mailing systems.

Enquiries should be made to:

Senior Education Officer, The Arts Council of Great Britain, 105 Piccadilly, London W1V 0AU.

Scottish Arts Council, 19 Charlotte Square, Edinburgh EH2 4DF.

Welsh Arts Council, Museum Place, Cardiff CF1 3NX.

Art teachers associations

There are many locally based associations for teachers who are interested in the visual arts. They are usually open to membership to teachers working in all levels of education. This can generate much useful work and contacts across the different phases. Their programmes will usually consist of a mixture of workshops, visits to schools, lectures, exhibitions and social events.

The names and addresses of the secretaries of these societies can usually be found in the LEA handbook. The national association for art teachers is NSEAD (see under separate entry).

British Film Institute

The British Film Institute serves a similar function to the Arts Council in the field of film and television. It has a well established educational programme and gives advice to teachers and schools about setting up courses and workshops in film-making, history of film and media studies.

Enquiries should be made to:

Head of Education Department, British Film Institute, 81 Dean Street, London W1.

Crafts council

Like the Arts Council, the Crafts Council exists to support and encourage work in the crafts through its sponsorship, through publications and exhibitions and through its education programme. Through the regional arts associations, it supports the placement of craftsmen and craftswomen in schools.

Enquiries should be made to:

Crafts Council, 12 Waterloo Place, London SW1Y 4AU.

In Wales, the Crafts Council works through the Crafts and Design Officer for the Welsh Arts Council. In Scotland, the crafts are dealt with by:

Scottish Development Agency, Small Business Division, 102 Telford Road, Edinburgh EH4 2NP.

Galleries

All the major London art galleries, and many of the provincial galleries, have education officers whose job it is to give teaching support to visiting schools. This support may consist of a combination of lecture programmes, teaching projects, provision of teaching materials (packs and worksheets) and general advice about how to use particular collections of works of art. Many gallery education officers design special programmes in association with particular exhibitions.

Enquiries should be made to the individual galleries.

In-service training

All local education authorities have a responsibility for providing programmes of in-service courses for their teachers. These will include one-day conferences and events, short courses and longer courses through secondment. In many authorities the programme of in-service training is supported and supplemented through the work of local teachers' centres.

All LEA courses are publicized through regular programmes and bulletins to schools and through teachers' centre programmes.

The department of Education and Science sponsors national in-service courses. The DES programme of short courses is sent to every school, as is the DES publication listing all those longer courses available through secondment to universities or colleges. These longer courses include opportunities to read for higher degrees, in which further study and research in art education is a major component.

Journals

'Arts Express' is published monthly and deals with matters of interest to teachers of the arts at all levels of education. Each month there are articles on the visual arts, dance, drama, music and literature in education. It is available through subscription from:

Arts Express, Subscriptions Dept, 43 Camden Lock, London NW1 8AF.

'Journal of Art and Design Education' is published termly by the National Society for Education in Art and Design. It provides an international forum for the dissemination of ideas, practical developments and research findings in art and design education at all levels of education. The journal is sent termly to all members of NSEAD (see below). Correspondence relating to subscriptions, back numbers etc. to:

Carfax Publishing Co., PO Box 25, Abingdon, Oxfordshire OX14 3UE.

'The Times Educational Supplement' publishes occasional supplements dealing with art, craft and design, in addition to being this country's major forum for articles, features, information and correspondence in all matters related to education.

Loan collections

Loan collections of works of art and craft are available through the museums and resources services of many LEAs (see below). Additionally, many of the regional arts associations have collections of works of art available for loan to schools and colleges (see below).

Some local museums and galleries are willing to loan work to schools from their reserve collections. Individual artists and local societies of artists are also often pleased to loan work for exhibition in schools.

Regional Arts Associations

The Regional Arts Associations advise on, promote and assess artistic provision in their region. They are independent organizations jointly funded by, and in working partnership with, the Arts Council and local authorities. Some have established specific policies to develop relationships with the education sector, and all provide information about arts activities of interest to those working in education.

Enquiries should be made through the Visual Arts Officer in the regions listed below:

Eastern Arts Association, 8–9 Bridge Street, Cambridge CB2 1UA.

East Midlands Arts, Mountfields House, Forest Road, Loughborough, Leics LE11 3HU.

Greater London Arts Association, 25–31 Tavistock Place, London WC1H 9SF.

Lincolnshire & Humberside Arts, St Hugh's, Newport, Lincoln LN1 3DN.

Merseyside Arts, Bluecoat Chambers, School Lane, Liverpool L1 3BX.

Northern Arts, 10 Osborne Terrace, Newcastle-upon-Tyne NE2 1NZ.

North West Arts, 12 Harter Street, Manchester M1 6HY.

Southern Arts, 19 Southgate Street, Winchester, Hampshire SO23 7EB.

South East Arts, 9–10 Crescent Road, Tunbridge Wells, Kent TN1 2LU.

South West Arts, Bradninch Place, Gandy Street, Exeter, Devon EX4 3LS.

South West Arts (Bristol office), 35 King Street, Bristol BS1 4DZ.

West Midlands Arts, Brunswick Terrace, Stafford ST16 1BZ.

Yorkshire Arts, Glyde House, Glydegate, Bradford BD5 0BQ.

Schools Curriculum Development Committee (SCDC)

The Schools Curriculum Development Committee was established in 1983 together with the Secondary Examinations Council to replace the Schools Council. The role of SCDC is 'to promote education by supporting curriculum development relevant to the needs of the schools in England and Wales'. SCDC has committed itself to work largely through supporting local curriculum development projects and working groups.

Teachers, working parties and institutions may submit proposals to SCDC for local research initiatives and request funding for these.

Enquiries should be made to:

SCDC, Newcombe House, 45 Notting Hill Gate, London W11 3JB.

Museums

All the major London museums and many provincial museums have education officers who provide similar services to those described in the section on galleries. Some museums have education officers, who are seconded to this work through their LEA. They may provide school rooms or workshop areas within the museum, where follow-up work to visits can take place and where there are collections of objects and artefacts for handling by the children.

Many museums are willing to lend artefacts to schools from their reserve collections, especially when these are requested in association with particular topics and where it is seen that such access encourages children to visit and use museums more frequently.

Museums and resource services

Many LEAs have museums or resources services which will deliver to schools a very wide range of resources and learning materials that are supportive to art education. These include: works of art and craft, reproductions of paintings, facsimiles of craft work, films, videos, slides, photographs, stuffed birds and animals, insects and butterflies.

Some museum and resource services provide collections or packs of material containing a variety of source material supportive to a particular project or programme of work, e.g. colour, surface, reflections, space etc.

National Society for Education in Art and Design

The National Society for Education in Art and Design was formed in 1984 through a merger of the National Society for Art Education with the Society for Education through Art. Membership is open to any teacher or lecturer who is interested in art education. The society is both a professional subject association and also provides trade union services and cover.

At national level it serves as a focal point for all matters related to art education and is represented on all the bodies and committees that deal with all matters related to art education. Through its districts it organizes conferences, workshops, exhibitions and social events.

'The Journal of Art and Design Education' is the society's main publication, which is sent termly to all members. In addition, the society publishes regular newsletters and occasional papers, and commissions works on matters of current interest in art education. Recent publications have dealt with careers in art and design and art education in primary schools.

Enquiries should be made to:

General Secretary, NSEAD, 7a High Street, Corsham, Wiltshire SN13 0ES.

Bibliography

Adams, E., and Ward, C. *Art and the Built Environment,* Longman.

Arnheim, R. *Art and Visual Perception,* Faber.

Association of Art Advisers. *Learning Through Drawing,* AAA.

Barrett, M. (1979) *Art Education: A Strategy for Course Design,* Heinemann.

Baynes, K. *Attitudes in Design Education,* Lund Humphries.

Berger, J. *Ways of Seeing,* BBC/Penguin.

De Bono, E. *Children Solve Problems,* Penguin.

DES. *Art in Secondary Schools 11–16,* HMSO.

Dubrey, F., and Willats, J. *Drawing Systems,* Studio Vista.

Eisner, E. *Educating Artistic Vision,* Collier-Macmillan.

Field, R. *Change in Art Education,* Routledge and Kegan Paul.

Gentle, K. *Children and Art Teaching,* Croom Helm.

Green, P. *Design Education: Problem Solving and Visual Experience,* Batsford.

Gregory, R. *Eye and Brain,* New English Library.

Gulbenkian Foundation. *The Arts in Schools,* Gulbenkian.

Koestler, A. *The Act of Creation,* Hutchinson/Pan.

Lowenfeld, V., and Brittain, W. L. *Creative and Mental Growth,* Collier Macmillan.

Ornstein, R. E. *The Psychology of Consciousness,* Jonathan Cape.

Read, H. *Education Through Art,* Faber and Faber.

Ross, M. *Arts and the Adolescent* (Schools Council Working Paper 54), Evans Methuen.

Ross, M. *The Creative Arts,* Heinemann.

Rowland, K. *Visual Education and Beyond,* Ginn.

Sausmarez, M. *Basic Design,* Studio Vista.

Schools Council. *Art 7/11* (Ed. R. Clement), Schools Council.

Schools Council. *Children's Growth Through Creative Experience,* Van Nostrand Reinhold.

Schools Council. *Visual Resources for Art Education 7/13* (Ed. D. Westall), Schools Council.

Vernon, M. D. *The Psychology of Perception,* Penguin.

Witkin, R. *The Intelligence of Feeling,* Heinemann.

Wooff, T. *Developments in Art Teaching,* Open Books.

INDEX